The Uncertain Future of American Public Higher Education

"Johnson kicks a hornet's nest of issues confronting our revered system of higher education. While various constituents of higher ed may be inclined to nitpick his litany of insights, they would do so at their collective peril. The unintended consequences of sticking with the status quo or tinkering at the margins could have dire effects. This is a clarion call for bold and innovative change."
—Lee Gorsuch, *President Emeritus, City University of Seattle, USA*

"*The Uncertain Future of American Public Higher Education* is a must-read for all of our country's higher education leaders, from university presidents, to governing boards, to state and federal policy makers. A former university president himself, Johnson draws on his many years of experience: first defending the status quo, then aggressively leading needed change and candidly identifying the sacred academic traditions that have created this crisis."
—Tom Brady, *Entrepreneur and Former Dean of Education at University of Toledo, USA*

"This thought-provoking book goes to the heart of why restructuring our entire education system is critical for our nation and our students' future. He shines a bright light on what changes need to be made."
—Bob Holden, *Governor of Missouri, 2001–2005*

"Dan Johnson articulates the necessity for a strong and effective higher education system by addressing the critical challenges it faces and offering potential solutions in the areas of leadership, planning, tuition, educational attainment, quality and efficiency, tenure, and intercollegiate athletics. This is a must read for policymakers, university presidents, politicians, journalists, university trustees and regents."
—James M. Tuschman, *Former Chairman, Ohio Board of Regents*

Daniel M. Johnson

The Uncertain Future of American Public Higher Education

Student-Centered Strategies for Sustainability

Daniel M. Johnson
University of Toledo
Toledo, OH, USA

ISBN 978-3-030-01793-4   ISBN 978-3-030-01794-1 (eBook)
https://doi.org/10.1007/978-3-030-01794-1

Library of Congress Control Number: 2018962745

© The Editor(s) (if applicable) and The Author(s) 2019
This work is subject to copyright. All rights are solely and exclusively licensed by the Publisher, whether the whole or part of the material is concerned, specifically the rights of translation, reprinting, reuse of illustrations, recitation, broadcasting, reproduction on microfilms or in any other physical way, and transmission or information storage and retrieval, electronic adaptation, computer software, or by similar or dissimilar methodology now known or hereafter developed.
The use of general descriptive names, registered names, trademarks, service marks, etc. in this publication does not imply, even in the absence of a specific statement, that such names are exempt from the relevant protective laws and regulations and therefore free for general use.
The publisher, the authors and the editors are safe to assume that the advice and information in this book are believed to be true and accurate at the date of publication. Neither the publisher nor the authors or the editors give a warranty, express or implied, with respect to the material contained herein or for any errors or omissions that may have been made. The publisher remains neutral with regard to jurisdictional claims in published maps and institutional affiliations.

Cover illustration: Oscar Spigolon; © z_wei/iStock/Getty Images Plus

This Palgrave Macmillan imprint is published by the registered company Springer Nature Switzerland AG
The registered company address is: Gewerbestrasse 11, 6330 Cham, Switzerland

For my life partner Elaine, my grandchildren—Megan, Dan, Owen and Maia—and the 42 million former college and university students struggling to pay off their student loans.

Preface

Each year the pressures on American higher education—particularly *public* higher education—continue to grow, challenging the major tenets, traditions and efficacy of the funding model, cost structures, faculty appointments and contracts, modes and delivery of education programs, and the social compact with students and their families. The staying power of these traditions have led to unaffordable costs for students, ineffective and inefficient delivery of instruction, and failure to adapt to advanced, lower cost, and more effective technologies and methods.

"The Uncertain Future" outlines the historic elements that constitute the fiscal, pedagogical, regulatory, administrative, and social infrastructure of public higher education and calls for education policy makers, university/college governing boards, the senior leadership of our institutions and governors to address and break with these anachronistic traditions for the benefit of students. Further, it calls on these same leaders of higher education to begin now to lay the foundation for a new higher education infrastructure, a new paradigm, that recognizes the importance and value of investing in human capital—our nation's students—and ridding the system of costly, ineffective outmoded traditions, unnecessary duplications of programs and services, and inefficient administrative structures.

American public higher education is in crisis, a crisis denied by many education leaders. Powerful vested interests have co-opted and are using our colleges and universities for pecuniary purposes and taking advantage of students for their own gain. Public confidence in higher education is waning and our universities are paying the price in decreasing public support, increasingly skeptical legislatures and lower enrollments in many colleges and universities. Righting the ship will take strong, collaborative leadership and a collective vision for a new path ahead that puts students first.

For decades, in my various roles in university administration, I came to know about most of these concerns and issues first hand. I heard the complaints from students and their parents and read the criticisms in the daily papers. And, like so many of my administrative colleagues, I was a defender and apologist for higher education with all its problems and challenges. My annual "state of the university" addresses highlighted our accomplishments and glossed over the many problematic "elephants in the room." I privately fought tuition increases but publicly defended them citing and justifying my position on the basis of inflation and the continuing cuts in state subsidies. I supported mandatory fees to sustain athletics and other programs that couldn't pay for themselves. In the safety of my home, I privately complained to my wife, Elaine, about my growing concerns, but on campus or in the community or at a conference, I defended the *status quo* as strongly as anyone. I thought that was my job.

Looking back on those years, continuing to watch and staying in touch with many of my colleagues in higher education, locally and nationally, I now believe I should have approached some of these issues differently. Rather than defend the *status quo* so strongly, I wish I had spoken out, expressed my concerns, and advocated more strongly for new policies or practices that, perhaps, could have slowed the decline or called attention to areas we as leaders in higher education needed to address.

This book is my attempt to give voice to these concerns, a voice that is decades late and, as my family might say, "A day late and dollar short." American higher education is increasingly burdened by its failure to address the growing inventory of major challenges. Our continuing acceptance and defense of practices, policies, and even a culture that is eroding the educational experience of what was once the finest system of higher education in the world are taking a debilitating toll on our colleges and universities.

"The Uncertain Future" is a call for leadership, reform, and a more student-centered approach to public higher education. Promoting a new perspective and the construction of a new paradigm for public higher education will require courageous leadership from our university presidents, enlightened trustees, and the informed commitment of education policy makers including state legislatures and especially the governors of our states. It desperately needs to happen, it can happen, and it will happen if the major stakeholders of higher education can find a way to work together toward a collective vision and collaborative leadership that puts students first.

Toledo, OH, USA   Daniel M. Johnson

Acknowledgements

Colleagues, friends, and family members have read, critiqued, and offered valuable suggestions for this book. I have drawn not only on their assistance and suggestions but, more importantly, on their encouragement and enthusiasm for the project. Jim Tuschman, former trustee of the University of Toledo and former chair of the Ohio Board of Regents, read the full manuscript and offered valuable suggestions only an attorney can provide. Tom Brady, former trustee of the University of Toledo, former dean of the UT Judith Herb College of Education, and fellow trustee at Lourdes University, read the manuscript and offered useful insights and suggestions. Lee Gorsuch, Chancellor during my years as Provost at the University of Alaska Anchorage, brought his lifetime of experience in higher education and his passion for education to his review of the manuscript.

I want to also express my appreciation to Milana Vernikova, editor at Palgrave-USA, for her patience, guidance, and support throughout the project. She helped make this book possible and, for that, I can't thank her enough.

This book would not have been possible without the many relationships I've been fortunate to have with faculty colleagues at several universities and my "bosses" including department chairs, deans, provosts, and presidents. I am especially grateful to Blaine Brownell, my provost at the University of North Texas back in the 1990s, good friend and colleague. Blaine gave me my first real job in administration and guided me through a rather steep learning curve.

For more than a half-century, I have had the good fortune to work with many outstanding trustees, donors, and public officials including several governors. I have also benefitted and learned from my relationship with students over the decades. Students, more than any other group, are the reason I wrote this book. They deserve better.

Most of all, I want to acknowledge and express my deep appreciation to my wife, Elaine. As with all my manuscripts, she read every word, often more than once, caught my many errors, offered suggestions, and encouraged me along the way. I am so very fortunate to have Elaine as my life partner.

Any errors of fact, interpretation, or presentation are mine.

Daniel M. Johnson

Contents

1	Introduction	1
2	Tuition Crisis: The Costs and Financing of Public Higher Education	11
3	Seat Time Academic Credit: What Does It Really Measure?	27
4	Tenure: Lifetime Employment in a Fast-Changing World	43
5	Campuses: Overvalued, Underused, and Very Costly	59
6	Lectures, Textbooks, Academic Calendar, and Administration: An Agenda for Change	75
7	Duplication of Programs: Where Do We Draw the Line?	91
8	Intercollegiate Athletics: Challenge to the Academic Mission	105

9	Presidential Selection, Salaries, and Moral Leadership	123
10	Student Demographics: The Coming Changes and Challenges for Higher Education	141
11	University Governance: Structures, Roles, and Responsibilities	157
12	Accreditation: How It Works and Is It Working?	175
13	Attacking the Problems: Student-Centered Strategies for Governors, Governing Boards, and University Presidents	193
14	Epilogue: Theoretical Perspectives on Change	209
Bibliography		215
Index		219

Acronyms

AAC&U   Association of American Colleges and Universities
AASCU   American Association of State Colleges and Universities
ACE   American Council on Education
AGB   Association of University Governing Boards
APPA   APPA-Leadership in Educational Facilities
CHEA   Council of Higher Education Accreditation
CIC   Council of Independent Colleges
NAICU   National Association of Independent Colleges and Universities
NASULGC Nationals Association of State Universities and Land Grant Colleges
SHEEO   State Higher Education Executive Officers

List of Tables

Table 2.1 Percentage reductions in state support for colleges and universities   14
Table 8.1 Football coaches' compensation exceeding one million dollars   108
Table 9.1 Media coverage of university failures   136

1

Introduction

The accelerating pace of societal change in the USA and globally is calling into question the stability, efficacy, and sustainability of institutions and social structures we have long taken for granted. One of those institutions happens to be among the most important, one upon which our economy and society depends i.e., the colleges and universities that make up our American system of higher education.

For more than a quarter century in senior leadership positions at several major universities, I've fought for, defended, and worked to strengthen the defenses of those universities against the pressures, challenges, and attacks that come from our critics, our legislatures, the media, and even some of our closest friends and donors. But these challenges to American higher education, no matter how strong our defenses, continue to grow stronger, louder, more threatening and are taking a toll that needs to be recognized, openly discussed, and addressed by the leaders of our institutions and policy makers at all levels.

Now, in my post-administrative days and more on the "outside looking in," I see these challenges from a different perspective, perhaps a little more clearly and certainly more holistically. Inside the administration, the problems and challenges made up my daily schedule and while these were always difficult they were seen as part of my job description as president; it was the world taken for granted. I took them one-at-a-time hoping to forestall a mini-crisis and to get through the workday in time to host a dinner with alums, donors, civic groups, or a campus guest. The general strategy was to break the problem into small pieces or units and work at solving or eliminating smaller, less-than-crisis challenges.

What I see today gives me much greater concern than when I was in the middle of it all. From this "outside" more holistic perspective, the cracks appear much larger, the current paradigm seems much weaker, and the sustainability of higher education, at least public higher education as we know it, is being called into question.

Unlike the nation's Liberty Bell with its single large crack, our system of public higher education and the paradigm that provides the conceptual, pedagogical, legal, regulatory, and financial structures for advanced learning and certification has multiple cracks—some large, some small—all seriously weakening the infrastructure, the very framework, and foundation upon which our public colleges and universities currently rest.

Given this picture, we must ask the obvious question: Is the current higher education paradigm sustainable? Am I misperceiving my old institutions and the system I fought to defend? Are we in a collective state of denial, whistling past the graveyard, hoping to hold out another year, another decade and pass this looming crisis on to the next generation of university leaders and higher education policy makers?

In his landmark essay, *The Structure of Scientific Revolutions* (1962), Thomas Kuhn,[1] elevated the concept of "paradigm" and brought it into the thinking and writings of the academy. Although Kuhn focused on the sciences, the strength of the paradigm concept has been shown applicable to other fields and disciplines. American higher education, viewed holistically, exhibits many of the characteristics of a paradigm. Kuhn and others have, for example, described paradigms in the following ways that apply to American higher education:

1 Introduction

> *Achievements, that for a time, provide a model...*
> *Concepts and practices that define a ...discipline at any particular time...*
> *Distinct, established patterns...*
> *common methods and standards that frame the object of interest...*
> *Examples of actual practice—*
> *which include law, theory, application, and instrumentation together—*
> *provide models from which spring particular coherent traditions...*
> *Commitment to the same rules and standards...*

The significance of Kuhn's work for this candid assessment of public higher education in the USA is the insight he provides into the way paradigms change. Paradigms do change, not only in science, as aptly described by Kuhn, but in other fields and disciplines. The achievements, practices, methods, standards, and models in any field, as in science, can and do shift with the pressures from new insights as well as the changing environmental context in which the field exists.

New discoveries, new knowledge, changing economics, new technologies, and even new ideologies can induce paradigm change. These changes, as Kuhn points out, can be constructive or destructive. With sufficient pressures from these changes, existing paradigms together with their standards, methods, rules, applications, and models are discarded, literally squeezed out, in favor of a new paradigm which more favorably embraces the changes. The failure of the existing paradigm—in this case, higher education—to meet the challenges of heightened expectations, negative public opinion, reduced legislative support, new delivery technologies, unacceptable cost–benefit ratios, and less attractive demographics bring substantial growing pressures for change. Kuhn's lesson applies: With the passage of time, anomalies accumulate within a field to the point that the entire paradigm itself is required to change to accommodate them. Structures and systems become anachronistic and can only sustain a limited amount of dissonance; when that limit is reached, structures and systems that make up the paradigm change or cease to be relevant. In Kuhn's parlance, this is a *paradigm shift*.

It is increasingly apparent from the rapidly expanding body of critical research, public opinion surveys, media coverage, and the agendas of higher education meetings, conferences, and associations that these anomalies and anachronistic features are bringing increased pressure and a paradigm shift is increasingly likely, if not imminent. Some argue that the shift is already well underway in American higher education. Clearly, the current higher education infrastructure lacks the strength it had a decade ago. Wave after wave of challenges and crisis after crisis are taking their toll. For many of those close to the front lines, there is the feeling that the dam is about to fail, that the twentieth-century structures, policies, subsidies, regulations, and programs that made possible the growth and development of American higher education in the twentieth century are failing in the twenty-first century and are in need of reconstruction and reform.

If we continue to apply Kuhn's insights, we might reasonably conclude that a paradigm shift is not a threat to the *need* for higher education, per se, but rather the manner and mode in which it is provided and continues to evolve. The current models, modes, and manners by which higher education functions, particularly *public* higher education, are costly, ineffectual and have been increasingly so for the past quarter century. The dissonance and dysfunctions are more evident every year with each new cohort of university students and every new budget cycle. The high cost of tuition and fees alone, with their annual increases outstripping inflation, is more than sufficient evidence of the failure of the system to meet the higher education needs of an ever-larger population. But the high cost of tuition is not the only dysfunction; it is only one of a myriad of challenges and pressures that are increasingly evident and are now *interacting* exacerbating the combined impact of these anomalies.

Among these challenges are the methods by which we measure university performance and account for its various functions; the growing chasm between the needs of the workforce, marketplace, and the curricula of our universities; the costly maintenance and growing obsolescence of our campuses; our failure to adopt effective teaching methods in favor of long-discredited modes; and the ancillary activities being added to the university experience that detract from learning and add to the costs students must pay or finance. These anomalies are bringing ever greater pressures that will, of economic and political necessity, bring a disruptive paradigm shift in American higher education. And that shift may well be underway.

These are *cracks* in the American paradigm of higher education that contribute to its very uncertain future. They are clearly visible to anyone reasonably close to or who cares about our nation's colleges and universities and the students they recruit every year. But this concern is not only about the impact of the costly dysfunctions on our universities and students; it is also about America's standing and leadership among other nations. It is about the demands of the knowledge economy and how we prepare future generations to find meaningful roles in an economy that is being driven by artificial intelligence, robotics, and the explosion of digitally based enterprises and industries.

It might be somewhat misleading or disingenuous to refer to these dysfunctions as *cracks* when clearly what was once a simple hairline fissure two or three decades ago has now become a huge hole or, worse, a gaping wound. Whatever the preferred metaphor, it is clear we have rapidly mounting problems that, if left unaddressed and unreformed, threaten not only the affordability and cost-effectiveness of American higher education for our nation's students but our leadership in the increasingly competitive international world of higher education. There is far too much at stake for future generations and our place in the world to ignore these huge cracks in the paradigmatic infrastructure upon which American higher education rests. There is an arms race in global higher education, and it can't be led or won using the inefficient, anachronistic systems, structures, and strategies of the 1950s and 1960s.

Every engaged educator and education policy maker knows there are countless issues and serious challenges confronting the higher education enterprise. There are those who argue that this is *normal* and par for the course. There are defenders of the *status quo* who argue that American higher education is fine, in great shape and the best is yet to come. They argue that higher education, as in every area of human endeavor, regularly encounters serious issues and challenges and this period of change and challenges is no different. We just have to stay the course, keep the present systems and structures in place, don't rock the boat, and continue learning how to "do more with less."

The purpose of this treatise is to respectfully take the strongest exception possible to this view. For the past two decades, we have witnessed changes and challenges that have gone far *beyond the normal* range of issues. The sheer scale, scope, and complexity of the issues defy resolution through normal channels. Even the systems and bureaucracies that have been put in place to address these issues have become or are becoming part of the problem scene.

These are the *anomalies* Kuhn describes as the antecedents of a paradigm shift.

The anomalies—I call them *cracks*—I'm most concerned with are the issues that challenge and frustrate the mission of higher education, that prevent significant parts of our population from gaining access to our universities, that threaten public support for the higher education enterprise, and that open the door to legitimate criticisms that undermine the moral authority of our colleges and universities. These cracks are patterns of institutional behavior that have evolved or developed in recent years that are, in some instances, inconsistent with democratic values and do not fit the ideals that enabled American universities and colleges to become the best in the world a half century ago.

Cracks usually begin as hairline creases barely visible to the average person or constituent. With the passage of a few years, this anomaly that many thought was a simple aberration and would disappear in time becomes the "new normal" and is soon taken for granted. The anomaly develops its own constituents with their vested interests, rationale, and justification for the maintenance of the new normal which may have little or no relationship with knowledge, learning, or the mission of higher education.

For the purposes of this treatise, I've identified a number of these issues and challenges, these cracks that are readily visible and that, taken together, threaten the capacity of our current infrastructure to provide for the sustainability of many of our colleges and universities and even our nation's current system of higher education. I've selected these anomalous characteristics based on my personal experiences as a forty-year veteran of higher education administration, the last ten years of which were in the most senior leadership positions at major universities. These cracks—anomalies that have become the "new normal" that now threaten America's higher education infrastructure—cut across the very fabric that holds our system together, i.e., tuition, credit hours, tenure, campuses, teaching, programs, textbooks, sports, salaries, demographics, governance, and accreditation.

These topics have played an important, long-term role and function in American higher education. They are terms and entities with which every student, faculty member, administrator, policy maker, and informed citizen are familiar. These elements constitute what many might consider the *core* or engine parts of higher education. These are the key elements of our system; they constitute the gears that make the higher education engine run. Each one, in its own way, is important; taken together, however, their dysfunctions and failures create a genuine crisis that can only be addressed through a major overhaul.

What is it about these elements of our higher education system—our paradigm—that qualifies them as cracks or anomalies that must be addressed? What is the rationale—the justification—for singling out these particular challenges? Why these and not others? To answer this question, I draw on my own experiences as a faculty member, department chair, dean, provost, and university president as well as my years leading a new university in the Middle East. Each of these issues seems to grow more problematic and difficult every year. Our solutions to these ever-growing problems are almost always focused on the symptoms, rarely the cause. We seem to have no capacity, power, or authority to solve the real problem; we deal only with symptoms.

To be honest, during my years in leadership roles, I did not—nor did my colleagues at the time—see these problems and issues as weaknesses in the system, much less anomalies in the higher education paradigm. We viewed—and blamed—most of the problems on ill-informed governors, legislators, bureaucrats, unions, and even our own university leaders. Looking back, it is much clearer that those were the hairline cracks in the 1990s and early 2000s that were not recognized as such but have now expanded to threaten the way we provide higher education and to whom we provide it.

Beyond my own experiences in university leadership roles, there are the policy and programmatic issues of our nation's higher education associations that validate these concerns as major issues. These associations represent the American higher education establishment and collectively pursue the maintenance of a collaborative policy environment that supports the *current* infrastructure. Even these conservative establishment associations are tackling, in their own ways, one or more of the anomalies threatening the sustainability of our colleges and universities.

A review of the websites, programs, and conference agendas of these associations—ACE, AASCU, APPA, AAC&U, AGB, CHEA, CIC, NAICU, NASULGC, SHEEO,[2] and others—provides a grand overview and inventory of the important issues and challenges they seek to address. Each of the issues that I now view as a serious challenge to the higher education paradigm, associations present as a topic at a conference, the task of a committee, an assignment to or job description for a member of the staff. These associations meet with and send letters to members of Congress outlining their collective concern and ask for their assistance if they think the problem is serious. Their missions, strategies, programs, and actions are geared to help keep the *current* paradigm working and, in all fairness, without the great work of these associations, the paradigm would have collapsed decades ago. But, the collapsing of the system, the breakup of the paradigm may be beyond the point of no return. The trajectory is clear. There is little the higher education associations can do that will stop the erosion. The forces of societal change are beyond their capacity to alter in any significant way. The higher education associations are, at best, a rearguard action.

If more justification is needed to accept these issues as cracks in the higher education paradigm, one need only to *Google* "crises in higher education." In addition to the hundreds of scholarly articles listed, there are scores of pages of references to a virtual library of material on the many crises in higher education, not only in the USA but in those nations that have modeled their systems after ours. I do not claim that the dozen or so issues that constitute the subject matter of this treatise are the only problems or anomalies challenging the infrastructure of American higher education. Those selected for this work are those that have been part of my experience, those that make up the agendas of our nation's higher education associations and, finally, those that form the basis of the growing body of crisis literature so prevalent and voluminous.

My hope is that we look at these challenges to our system of higher education for what they really are; they are clear signals that we must find a new way, a new course, and a new mode and paradigm for meeting the higher education and research needs of our nation's population, workforce, and marketplace.

References

1. Thomas Kuhn, *The Structure of Scientific Revolutions* (University of Chicago Press, 1962).
2. See Acronyms for names of associations.

2

Tuition Crisis: The Costs and Financing of Public Higher Education

"Beyond the reach of the middle class." This is a phrase you can find in literally hundreds of articles that have been written about the soaring tuition rates over the past decade. Even our public universities—a bargain compared to most private institutions—are increasingly beyond the reach of many of those who most need a college education as a way out of poverty, minimum wage and dead-end jobs. Lacking resources, information, and understanding of their options, middle-class kids and those from lower socio-economic situations turn to the many lending institutions all too ready and eager to provide student loans, semester after semester until graduation if the students are fortunate enough to complete their studies. Sadly, the pressures of financial stress and family responsibilities combined with the academic workload from classes delay graduation for many an additional year or two turning a traditional 4-year degree into a five, six, or seven year degree. For many, the obstacles are just too large resulting in dropout rates that exceed 50% or more in some states.

The hidden tragedy in this scenario being played out all across the nation is a growing population of young people who have borrowed tens of thousands of dollars to pay for tuition, mandatory fees, and books but who fail to complete their degrees and reap the advantage of increased compensation that comes with graduation that enables them to repay these student loans. Barely half of those who enroll actually complete their degrees in six years or less.

This is a tragic tale that is being retold on a daily basis. I've been with undergraduate and graduate students and listened to the stories about their loans, their indebtedness and their fears about the future. I recently talked to a graduate student finishing his Master's degree in education. He had borrowed $70,000 so far for both his undergraduate and graduate studies and still had a semester to complete the requirements for his degree. Part of his story was that he was also assisting his parents—an immigrant family—through this period. He was engaged to marry a young lady—also a student—who had borrowed "a lot of money." I can imagine that their combined indebtedness could easily exceed $100,000; at this point neither the graduate student nor his fiancee had a job nailed down. My student friend was now—perhaps for the first time—facing the stark reality of his financial situation and future of indebtedness.

In addition to my personal knowledge of students with these huge loans, there are countless stories in the popular press, periodical literature, and scholarly journals documenting the tragic financial situation of a growing proportion of today's graduates. It is one of the indisputable facts about higher education in the USA that has turned what was—and should be—a sense of great accomplishment for graduates into a time of reckoning and sober reflection on the price they paid for their college degree. For the first time in my experience, I am hearing students question whether the degree was worth the price. Sadly, the voices of those questioning the value and cost of a college education are growing louder. Many are opting out or dropping out altogether.

Anyone who has looked at this state of affairs quickly learns that the high cost of higher education and the problem of student loans and indebtedness is complex with its causative tentacles reaching back to rising inflation, institutional practices, education policies, government programs, competition among universities for students, availability of easily obtained loans, and even deceptive practices among some of the institutions involved. It truly is a very complex problem the results of which millions of young people will be living with for decades.

There is no silver bullet nor simple solution to what has become one of the most serious and complex problems in American higher education. The seriousness of this problem and its financial and psychological impact on a generation of students and graduates, with no solution in sight, combined with the drag it creates on local economies has weakened our nation's system of higher education and for the first time begs the question of the cost/benefit of a college degree. The high cost of higher education and the resulting student loan problem has, for a growing proportion of young people—mostly from lower income and blue-collar families—cast doubt on the affordability and even the wisdom of pursuing a college degree.

Over the past decade, I have talked with many students, parents, and interested citizens about the high cost of higher education. Most want to know *why* it costs so much. Parents and grandparents frequently recount how inexpensive it was for them in the 1960s, 1970s, and 1980s making it possible to work their way through college without leaving them in debt. Everyone recognizes the impact of inflation and accepts that as a factor; what they don't understand is why and how the cost of higher education has far outstripped inflation. "What," they ask, "is going on? We just don't understand how this can be. Please explain it to us. Please, just tell us the truth."

My response to these students and their parents reflects what we know about the rapid increase in tuition and the cost of public higher education in the USA over the past two decades. The increases are the result of two significant arithmetic changes: One is the *additions* to university programs, services, amenities, facilities, technologies, and salaries. The second is the *subtractions* of state support at public universities. Widespread reductions in public support for state universities combined with the rising costs of remaining competitive have forced universities to find needed resources in the only other renewable source available, i.e., student tuition.

But there is much more to the rising cost of higher education than the arithmetic changes of additions and subtractions. Those who seek to fully understand the factors at work in the economics of tuition and the interplay of these factors soon grasp the complexity of the quest. Beyond the many factors at work and their interplay are the complexities of the decision-making processes that result in heightened tuition rates. Who makes these decisions and why do they make them when it is fully understood that increased tuition rates translate into larger loans and deeper debt for students?

Major Drivers of Tuition Increases

Reductions in State Support. The principal driver of escalating tuition over the past four decades has been the retreat of state legislatures and governors from their historic support for higher education. The magnitude of these reductions in state support for public colleges and universities has precluded any reasonable chance of maintaining the tuition levels of the early 1970s and retaining the quality and number of programs without new sources of revenue to offset these cuts.

Nationally, state support for higher education in 1975 provided approximately 60% of the revenue for state colleges and universities; by 2010, periodic reductions brought the state support to 34%. According to American Council on Education (ACE),[1] many public universities had their state support cut by more than half during this period, some by nearly 70%. States with highest percentage reductions in support for their colleges and universities are presented in Table 2.1.

Notwithstanding some relief from cuts and even a few increases in recent years, state spending and support for higher education remains "below historic levels" according to a 2017 report from the Center on

Table 2.1 Percentage reductions in state support for colleges and universities

Colorado	69.4%
South Carolina	66.8
Rhode Island	62.1
Arizona	61.9
Oregon	61.5
Minnesota	55.8
Virginia	53.6
Vermont	51.3

Budget and Policy Priorities.[2] Authors of the report, Michael Mitchell, Michael Leachman, and Kathleen Masterson, reveal that state funding for public two-year and four-year institutions in the school year ending in 2017 was nearly $9 billion below the 2008 level, after adjusting for inflation. The impact of these reductions was predictable and is now a reality:

> At a time when the benefit of a college education has never been greater, state policymakers have made going to college less affordable and less accessible to the students most in need…[they add] …state lawmakers must renew their commitment to high-quality, affordable public higher education by increasing the revenue these schools receive. By doing so, they can help build a stronger middle class and develop the entrepreneurs and skilled workers needed for a strong state economy.[3]

Administrative Costs and Growth. Theories and explanations for tuition growth abound: indeed, the "truths" behind tuition increases depend on who is asking and, the answers can differ considerably depending on who is answering. For example, Robert Reich, former Secretary of the US Department of Labor, believes the costs of higher education are being driven by overspending on amenities and university bureaucracies that have "become too large and redundant." Reich's view is "You don't need that many administrators."[4]

However, if you ask James Duderstadt, former President of the University of Michigan, he will tell you that one of the "great myths" concerning the high cost of higher education is "universities spend too much money on administration." "Nothing," he says, "could be further from the truth." And, goes on to add "…the American university has a very thin administration—actually precariously thin in view of the increasing complexity and accountability of these institutions."[5]

This is not a new debate. The lines in this debate were drawn decades ago and were clearly articulated in a 1991 report by AAUP on "Administrative Bloat." The author of the lead article in the AAUP report, Barbara R. Bergmann, distinguished professor of economics at American University, leaves little doubt or much to the imagination on her position:

Undetected, unprotested, and unchecked, the excessive growth of administrative expenditures has done a lot of damage to life and learning on our campuses. On each campus that suffers from this disease, and most apparently do, millions of dollars have been swallowed up. Huge amounts have been devoted to funding administrative positions that a few years ago would have been thought unnecessary.

If it were just a matter of the money wasted, that would be bad enough. But the bloating of college administrations over the past decades has made administrative performance worse rather than better. It has bogged us down in reels of time-consuming and despair-creating red tape. It has fostered delusions of grandeur among some of the administrative higher-ups, whose egos have grown along with the size of the staffs under their supervision.[6]

Concerns with the size and growth in university administrations as a factor, if not a major driver in the escalating cost of higher education, continue to mount to this day. The relevance of the expansion of university administrations to rising costs, however, depends on whether the responder is an inside member of a university administration or an outsider. Further, these very different perspectives also strongly suggest that any reform of university bureaucracies will not come from the embedded, bureaucratically structured administrations; reform and restructuring of the way we administer universities and higher education will need to come from governors, legislatures, and education policy makers, boards of trustees and donors.

One of the areas of major administrative redundancies for many states is the central college/university systems offices. Central systems offices which, in theory, provide greater efficiencies through consolidated fiscal operations, legal services, personnel services, information technology, insurance, purchasing, and other services have themselves been the source of inefficiencies, duplication, and costly redundancies.

Critics of such systems have been pointing to this duplication of administrative costs for decades arguing that these offices replicate work done on the campuses and employ scores of bureaucrats who have no direct role in teaching, research, or service at the universities.[7] Texas, for example, operates six systems offices employing nearly 2000 in 2014.

The University of California and California State University systems employ over 3000. Even small states such as Alaska—the smallest in terms of colleges and universities—have evolved large, powerful systems offices; University of Alaska System employed 263 in 2014 even though the Alaska system is made up of only two small-to-moderate size universities in Fairbanks and Anchorage and one very small university in Juneau. One community college and a scattering of small branch campuses make up the rest of the system. The services at the system office largely duplicate those on the campuses and add substantially to the cost of education for students and taxpayers. The costs for operating university systems offices range considerably from an average of approximately $500 to a whopping $3336 per student.[8]

These costs often raise serious accountability issues and problems for states that ultimately impact the cost of tuition and the financial burden of students. For example, a recent state audit of the California State University System found that the system "could not sufficiently explain why it needed all the new managers, including deans, head coaches, and vice presidents among other positions." The report reveals that for an eight-year period ending in 2016, the system had a growth rate for full-time managers that exceeded the growth rate for faculty and non-faculty support staff. Equally important, the audit reported "the system's 23 campuses did not have policies for periodically comparing their spending levels or reviewing their budget limits."[9]

The rapid growth in the cost and staffing of university administrations nationally in recent decades raises many questions and serious concerns of accountability at a time when universities, more than ever, need to have the trust of students, families, and taxpayers that they are operating as efficiently as possible. Most public universities, however, are seriously challenged by the need to operate efficiently when it comes to administrative costs. Governors, legislatures, governing boards, and education policy makers have an opportunity, indeed, a responsibility to reduce administrative costs and improve institutional efficiency in the interest of slowing the rise of student tuition.

Financial Aid as a Driver of Increasing Tuition. One of the continuing controversies in higher education is the argument that increases in financial aid have been a major driver of increased tuition. The argument began in 1987 when then-Secretary of Education William Bennett wrote an op-ed piece for the *New York Times* entitled "Our Greedy Colleges"[10] in which he asserts that increases in federal financial aid allow colleges to "blithely...raise their tuition, confident that federal loan subsidies would help cushion the increase." The *New York Times* piece now called the "Bennett Hypothesis," sparked waves of criticism and support as well as three decades of studies seeking to prove or disprove Bennett's proposition.

The ACE is among those that argued forcefully against the claims that increases in federal student aid are driving increases in college tuition: Such claims, they argue, are "empirically unsupported." For ACE, the "bottom line is that there is no evidence—and certainly no conclusive data—to suggest that federal student aid significantly affects college prices. None, zero, zip, nada."[11]

Among those seeking to resolve the controversy, the Federal Reserve Bank of New York took up the question and studied the impact of the 2006 congressionally approved increase in the maximum subsidized loan a student could borrow by $1000. After controlling for the influence of other factors, the researchers estimated "for every additional dollar of subsidized loans made available to students, institutions increased their sticker tuition about 60 cents." The results were greatest at the expensive for-profit and private nonprofit colleges. Critics of the study point to the short period of time covered by the researchers and the significant discounts that accompany price increases.[12]

Notwithstanding these opposing positions, many observers of higher education continue to suspect and believe that open-ended subsidies—Parent PLUS loan program—and other easy-to-obtain student loans create a temptation and motivation for colleges to raise tuition. Some argue, "Why not? Students can get the money they need to attend... and we need it. Why not raise tuition?"

Recent research published by the National Bureau of Economic Research, sought to test various explanations for the steep rise in college tuition between 1987 and 2010. The study tested "supply-side" forces, "demand-side" forces and macroeconomic forces. Their quantitative research model demonstrates that the "combined effects" of these forces more than account for the tuition increases and reveal important insights into the role of individual factors in explaining tuition increases. The "model suggests demand-side theories have the most predictive power. In fact," the researchers conclude, "our results show the Bennett hypothesis can fully account for the tuition increase on its own."[13]

Thinking about federal assistance, financial aid, and college loan programs put in place to help students attend college following the huge losses of state support, I'm reminded of the oft-quoted phrase attributed to Clare Boothe Luce, "*No good deed goes unpunished.*" This could easily apply to the student financial aid industry that expanded numerous forms of aid to students—"a good deed"—one of the consequences of which was significantly increased tuition rates, i.e., "punishment." Clearly, the "system" has failed and the results of this failure are the massive trillion-plus dollar student loan debt now being carried by the nation's young adults.

The Amenities War. One of the most important but largely unreported stories in American higher education in the past half decade is the growing competition among colleges and universities for students. This increased competition for students is largely due to the changing population structure with smaller numbers in traditional college age cohorts and composition changes reflecting the growing population subgroups that have lower-than-average college-going rates. Combine these demographic changes with one of the longest periods of economic expansion and you have a recipe for fewer college-going students. Fewer college-going students translate into much keener competition among colleges and universities for student applications and admissions.

This competition has become increasingly fierce and has evolved into an all-out "arms race" as thousands of colleges and universities across the nation aggressively seek to attract and maintain student enrollments. Many colleges and universities are literally scrambling to recruit enough students to meet projected budget expenditures, much of which is in the form of fixed costs. The increased competition has led colleges and universities to keep adding amenities—often on borrowed money—to increase their attractiveness to students and families. Fearful of declining enrollment and losing tuition dollars, colleges feel increasing pressure to construct expensive, often luxurious facilities, to compete for students. Most of these new facilities are non-academic and do not add to the quality of education or the university.

In some instances, universities seek the approval of students to add new fees to secure loans or bonds to pay for these new facilities. For most of these projects, students who vote generally graduate or leave the university before the new facility or amenity is finished; those who end up paying for the facility have had little or no "say" in the decision. And, it is not uncommon that the student fees approved for the project do not fully cover the continuing costs of the new facility forcing the administration to draw funds from other sources including the operating budget.

The current trend of adding new facilities, recreational amenities, and entertainment venues as well as upscale residential and dining complexes as a way of attracting students and growing enrollments has added to the costs at many universities that must be paid for by students. To make matters worse, there are increasing numbers of colleges and universities where adding the new amenities and upscale facilities have not produced the enrollment growth or sustainability for which it was built. The result is often fewer students paying larger fees to cover the cost of the facility and making the college or university even less attractive financially than before.

Redundant student health-care costs. One unexpected area driving higher costs to students is through what is described by Keybridge Research as "unnecessary and redundant health care costs." They report that while most students have health insurance through their parents coverage, they discover in many instances that such insurance "has little value on college campuses." They also report that "most students with private insurance are forced to pay redundant student health fees." For the typical student, the additional costs over four years amount to well over $1200.[14] This is, clearly, a correctable problem.

Other Drivers of Tuition. In addition to the major "drivers" of heightened tuition, there are other practices known to be influencing these increases in recent years. Strangely enough, there is the view—not all that uncommon—that somehow "price reflects quality." Governing boards have been known to raise tuition motivated by the psychology of pricing that higher tuition means a higher quality educational experience. Interestingly, there are instances where increased tuition rates resulted in increases or even "spikes" in enrollment. All one can say is, *caveat emptor.*

Colleges and universities are also very conscious of the tuition pricing by their chief competitors. If one or more competitors of a university increases tuition, it is believed that they have license to increase their tuition, accordingly. Or, as one recent report put it, "When one raises tuition, others feel they have the permission to do the same."

Reducing services or enacting "fee for service" policies have had the effect of increasing student costs at many universities. Services, events, and activities that were provided to students free or the costs covered by a general student fee are no longer covered requiring out-of-pocket payment by students. These policy changes, in effect, increase the overall cost of attending college or university.

Adding to the students' costs are the efforts by university administrations to generate maximum profits from operations and auxiliary enterprises such as dining halls, bookstores, and parking. These added profits are paid by students and are often added to the amount for which they seek student loans.

The System Is Broken

The impact of the "tuition crisis" is being felt daily in the lives of more than 42 million people. These are the former college and university students who borrowed more than $1.3 trillion to finance their education. They are now the debtors in hock to Wall Street and the federal government. Most people are acutely aware of the crisis from the media coverage it has drawn and many know one or more of these former students repaying their loans, with interest.

What is not widely known is the financial windfall student loans are creating for those who make these loans, i.e., Wall Street and the federal government. The student loan business, with its origin in a federal government program—National Defense Education Act (NDEA) of 1958—has grown to become one of the biggest banking industries in history. The political history of the student loan industry with its roots in NDEA and fully institutionalized by President Lyndon Johnson in 1965 as the Higher Education Act to help make college possible for everyone is a history of privatization that has been generating hundreds of millions of dollars in interest and profits for the holders of these loans. James B. Steele and Lance Williams, in their article on the history of student loans, "Who Got Rich off the Student Debt Crisis?"[15] describe how this evolved: "Step by step," they write, "Congress has enacted one law after another to make student debt the worst kind of debt for Americans – and the best kind for banks and debt collectors."

Equally concerning is the current role of the federal government, described by Steele and Williams as "one of the winners in the profit spree behind this debt." By their assessment, based on the Department of Education's calculations, "…the government earns in some years an astounding 20 percent on each loan." Making their point, they quote Senator Elizabeth Warren (D-Mass); speaking on the floor of the Senate, Warren said the US government "turns young people who are trying to get an education into profit centers to bring in more revenue for the federal government. This is obscene. The federal government should be helping students get an education—not making a profit off their backs."[16]

The financing of public higher education in the USA has become deeply politicized. It has also become one of the few issues that connect with local, state, and national interests. The 2016 Presidential Election, for example, had candidates for the first time openly proposing "free tuition" for community colleges and even four-year universities. Candidates with more conservative platforms proposed reforms in the student-debt repayment options making it easier to repay with fewer defaults.

Some states have tried to address the problem but most of these efforts have proven to be mere band-aids for very critical, even life-threatening wounds in the system. One politically convenient strategy is freezing tuition at state universities. Freezing tuition, however, is a legislative strategy that often inflicts more damage to the universities than it solves for the students; usually, these tuition-freeze policies come with reduced subsidies thereby lowering the ability of the institutions to cover rising costs and remain competitive.

A few states have attempted to roll back tuition rates but the amount of the reductions—as welcomed as it is to students and families—fails to alter the student loan equation to any significant degree. Tuition rollbacks cannot succeed, however, without reinstating lost subsidies to their 1980s level. The likelihood of that happening is near zero.

What is not well understood or even discussed by policy makers is the impact of the student tuition debt on local and regional economies. The impact of that indebtedness on the economies of our cities and states is huge when you consider that these loans prevent young people from buying cars, houses, appliances, take vacations, and engage in the kind of spending that keeps our neighborhoods and towns in business. Our high tuition rates are preventing states and the nation from reaping the benefits of our investment in higher education. Economically, it makes no sense to invest in a higher education system that produces debt-laden graduates who can't afford to take financial advantage of the degrees they've spent four, five, or six years or more to earn.

The high cost of public higher education and the problems of financing these costs, the mounting mandatory fees, room, and board and all of the associated costs have ruptured our nation's system higher education. These problems are well known and have been well documented for a decade or longer. The business model for public higher education is broken and the current paradigm is unsustainable. And, we know very well that this requires a fix. So far, however, few education leaders and policy makers, legislatures and governors have shown the interest, courage and will necessary to address the problem and/or its causes.

Sadly for Americans, other nations are beginning to lead the way, investing in higher education at levels that allow any qualified student to attend university at reasonable or even no cost. And, on closer examination, it is evident that they are getting better results from their investments. The Georgetown Center on Education and the Workforce has comparative data on national investment in higher education. Their assessment is the USA devotes more of our economy to postsecondary education than any other developed country (we tied with South Korea), but we ranked near the bottom in efficiency or degrees earned by percentage of GDP spent.[17]

Our standing in the global higher education marketplace as measured by the size of our investment is not threatened. What is threatening is the way we pay for it and what we get in return for that investment.

Conclusions

The picture of higher education in America increasingly features growing student indebtedness that has long-since surpassed the trillion dollar mark and is well on the way to two trillion dollars. The human impact of that indebtedness is growing, life-altering, demoralizing and, for many, lifelong. The economic paradigm for higher education is also failing our colleges and universities forcing many leaders and governing boards to invest in marketing strategies rather than strategies that strengthen academic programs and learning. The financing model for higher education based on student debt, while producing windfall profits for Wall Street lending organizations, is also having an adverse impact on local economies. Student loan payments preclude other purchases that help keep local economies healthy.

There are few, if any, problems in our nation's institutions of higher education that are more serious or better documented. It is the issue of greatest concern to university leaders and policy makers. More importantly, it is of even greater concern to parents of high school-age children who see no way—other than debt—to pay for their children's college education. Governors, legislatures, governing boards, and university leaders must find and create a more affordable, efficient, effective, and sustainable paradigm.

References

1. American Council on Education, *State Funding: Race to the Bottom* (Winter 2012).
2. Michael Mitchell, Michael Leachman, and Kathleen Masterson, *A Lost Decade in Higher Education Funding* (Center on Budget and Policy Priorities, August 23, 2017).

3. Ibid., p. 1.
4. Mark I. McNutt, "Why Does College Cost So Much?" *U.S. News* (September 22, 2014).
5. James J. Duderstadt, *A University for the 21st Century* (Ann Arbor: University of Michigan Press, 2000), 173.
6. Barbara R. Bergmann, "Bloated Administrations, Blighted Campuses," *Academe* (Volume 77, 1991), 12–16.
7. Jon Marcus, "The Reason Behind Colleges' Ballooning Bureaucracies," *The Atlantic* (October 6, 2016).
8. National Center for Higher Education Management Systems, Survey, 2010–11.
9. *Chronicle of Higher Education* (April 20, 2017).
10. William Bennett, "Our Greedy Colleges," *New York Times* (February 18, 1987).
11. Bryan J. Cook and Terry W. Hartle, *Myth: Increases in Federal Student Aid Drive Increases in Tuition* (American Council on Education, Spring 2012).
12. Amy Scott, *Does Financial Aid Really Drive Up Tuition?* (Marketplace, December 14, 2016).
13. Gordon Grey and Aaron Hedlund, *Accounting for the Rise in College Tuition* (National Bureau of Economic Research, February 2016).
14. Keybridge Research LLC, *Unnecessary & Redundant Health Care Costs for College and University Students* (November 12, 2009).
15. James B. Steel and Lance Williams, "Who Got Rich Off the Student Debt Crisis," *RevealNews.org* (June 28, 2016).
16. Ibid.
17. Jordan Weissmann, "America's Wasteful Higher Education Spending," *The Atlantic* (September 2013).

3

Seat Time Academic Credit: What Does It Really Measure?

The semester credit hour is the "currency" of higher education. It is the number that measures a student's course load and goes on their transcript when they have successfully completed a class. It is the measure used to determine when a student has met and satisfied the criteria for a degree. It is also the unit by which faculty workloads are determined and measured. The number of semester credit hours produced by public universities is the number submitted to their states that determines the amount of subsidy the university receives. It is also the number used by university administrations to help determine the size of college and departmental budgets. And, it is the unit used by accrediting bodies to help measure institutional productivity.

As a measure of students' course loads, faculty workloads, budgets for colleges and departments, the flow of dollars from state coffers to the bank accounts of public universities as well as a tool for assessing institutional productivity, semester credit hours have become the basis of daily schedules and workloads, institutional accounting and the economic infrastructure that allows colleges and universities to function. There are very few, if any, metrics more important to the operation of higher education, particularly public higher education, than the semester credit hour.

© The Author(s) 2019
D. M. Johnson, *The Uncertain Future of American Public Higher Education*,
https://doi.org/10.1007/978-3-030-01794-1_3

Considering the importance of academic credit for managing all the major transactions of a college or university, one would assume the credit hour is a valid and reliable measure of *education* or learning. On closer examination, however, it is abundantly clear that the semester credit hour, as it is operationalized and used, measures neither education nor learning. The rationale for its continued use is almost totally pragmatic, i.e., we can't seem to come up with anything better that would provide the functional equivalent that actually measures what we claim is our mission and purpose, i.e., learning, knowledge, and education.

Surprisingly, many who regularly use the semester credit hour for their university work—students, faculty, staff, administrators, state bureaucrats, and policy makers—have little understanding of its history, true meaning or what it actually measures. John Harris[1] has studied the American academic credit system tracing its roots back to the 1700s. Harris's work reveals how the nation's first universities relied on oral examinations—sometimes public examinations—to determine a student's qualifications for a degree. The assumption was that students acquired "a sum of knowledge which tended to unify and coalesce into a related whole" that could be assessed by qualified examiners through oral examinations. There was a general consensus that the exams, "should be 'rigid, and extend to the whole of collegiate literature' and only those found 'well skilled in the liberal arts and sciences' should be given degrees." At Yale, as at other colonial colleges, students were "called up singly and each examined orally." Harris writes that this "display of learning made quite a public appeal and remained popular till well into the nineteenth century."[2]

By mid-nineteenth century, however, the popular oral and often public examination gave way to written examinations. The rationale for the change from public oral examinations to written examinations was the view that "much greater equity" could be assured with written examinations. The move to written exams, not surprisingly, was not without its critics who "were not so much the advocates of the public exhibition as the defenders of the recitation." They argued that daily recitation "was an examination itself." The debate over oral examinations, recitation, and written examinations gathered steam in the nineteenth century with college leaders weighing in on the issues.

Harvard President Charles Eliot was among the more outspoken of those in this late nineteenth-century debate. He argued that it was a mistake to "join the teaching and examining function in the same person because, while such a practice might provide a measure of the learning done, it afforded no satisfactory measure of teaching."[3] These positions and arguments by Eliot and other prominent education leaders helped to elevate the importance and visibility of this issue.

Eliot pursued other innovations and reforms he wanted to bring to higher education. One was the notion of "electives" that would allow students to pursue areas of interest that were outside the structured curriculum. He went so far as to eliminate required courses. He needed a way to recognize the elective courses and saw the contact hour as a useful measure and solution to this problem.

The late 1800s and early 1900s became an important transition period in education. Leaders faced a growing list of problems as the number of students increased and new colleges and institutions of learning were sprouting up in nearly every region of the young nation. In addition to the issue of examinations, questions of standards, calendars, qualifications of teachers, and teacher training gained attention and prompted widespread discussions and debates. Even the distinction between high school and college was not clearly defined which added to the growing list of issues needing resolution.

The growth of secondary and higher education required an ever increasing number of teachers and professors. The education professions were not well organized nor were salaries attractive to those who might possess the qualifications for the classroom or professoriate. The compensation problem was exacerbated by lack of a pension program for retiring teachers.

It was during this period that industrialist Andrew Carnegie took a strong interest in advancing education. Drawing on his vast resources, Carnegie established a pension program for college faculty but insisted that institutional eligibility for participation in the program required meeting certain standards, e.g., number of full-time faculty, definition of "full-time," courses of instruction, admissions requirements and others. This required a method to measure eligibility standards that most or all institutions would recognize and adopt. The Carnegie Unit became that measure. In a very short period of time, the Carnegie Unit became widely accepted as the basis for granting high school diplomas and credit hours toward the baccalaureate and helped clarify the blurry distinction between secondary and higher education.[4]

Known today as the credit hour, the Carnegie Unit became the basic measuring tool for determining students' readiness for college and their progress through an acceptable program of study. Colleges, needing a system to track student progress toward a degree, began measuring the teaching of subject matter in credit-hour units. The value of each course in high school and in college was listed in units of credit, and institutions adopted policies that stated how many units or credit hours were required for receiving the respective degrees. The utility of the Carnegie Unit or credit hour was quickly recognized and was described as "the building block of modern American education serving as the foundation for everything from daily school schedules to graduation requirements, faculty workloads, and eligibility for federal financial aid." The credit hour remains today "the central organizing feature of the vast American education system, from elementary school to graduate school."[5]

Almost from the beginning of its adoption more than a hundred years ago, the Carnegie Unit, the precursor to the semester credit hour, had its critics and has remained controversial to the present day. This controversy takes on even greater importance in today's higher education economy as we strive to establish greater accountability, adapt to the rapidly expanding areas of knowledge and technology as well as create a much-needed closer alignment between education and the needs of our workforce, economy, and society.

All of this begs the question: Why is the semester credit hour controversial? The simple answer is it equates learning and knowledge with time. The flaw and growing concern is the fundamental criterion of the credit hour, i.e., "the amount of time spent on a subject, not the results attained." As the USA and other nations move ever closer to knowledge-based economies, *knowledge* must become the "currency" of higher education, not time sitting in a classroom or in front of a computer screen. The challenge for educators is operationalizing knowledge. With a time-based measure, the problem is simple: How much time do students spend in class or in front of their computer screen or tablet? At best, time in class—seat time—becomes a poor, invalid, and unreliable surrogate or measure for knowledge and learning. Time spent in class measures nothing more than time spent in class.

For more than a century, legitimate critics of the Carnegie Unit and semester credit hour have argued against a *time-based* measure of learning and knowledge. Abbott L. Lowell, Eliot's successor at Harvard, is said to have spent a great deal of his presidency "undoing the havoc wrought on the college by Eliot's' system." Lowell is quoted as saying "One of the most serious evils of American education in school and college is counting by courses – the habit of regarding the school or college as an educational savings bank where credits are deposited to make up the balance required for graduation, or for admission to more advanced study."[6]

The weakness of the semester credit-hour accounting system goes far beyond counting courses. The credit-hour accounting system is the basis for measuring nearly every service and function of today's universities. Reid Kisling, consultant to the American Association of Collegiate Registrars and Admissions Officers, said, "It's hard to imagine what we report that isn't credit based."[7] Like any currency, the credit-hour accounting system has worked for a century because, it has been accepted, even with its spurious nature, by the major users of the system. Acceptance by major users does not, however, lend validity or reliability to the credit hour as a measure of learning or knowledge. It is, at best, "a crude proxy for student learning." It is this crude proxy or, more accurately, this disconnect between the credit hour and learning or knowledge that is driving the movement for reform.

In addition to the individual and organizational critics of "seat time" or time-based academic credit that have challenged the system for more than a hundred years, the organization most closely associated with the architect of the system, The Carnegie Foundation for the Advancement of Teaching, has continued its participation in the ongoing discussions of the credit unit. Recognizing the importance and intense scrutiny of the credit unit as a measure of academic performance, the Foundation conducted its own assessment of the current system. The results, published in 2015, were significant and constitute the strongest criticism yet of the Carnegie Unit, i.e., *The Carnegie Unit: A Century-Old Standard in a Changing Education Landscape.*[8]

The Foundation's two-year study captures the century-long critical history of the credit unit but more importantly places their concerns in the context of today's needs and challenges. The Foundation report concludes with the following:

> After studying the Carnegie Unit's relationship to today's reforms, we have concluded that American education's reliance on the Carnegie Unit is an impediment to some of the solutions sought by reformers. Most notably, the federal government's financial aid rules requiring colleges and universities to measure student progress using Carnegie Units are a barrier to the spread of flexible delivery models in higher education.[9]

This is not the first expression of the Foundation's concerns regarding the credit unit: This is a long-standing dilemma. Carnegie Foundation President Henry Suzzallo wrote of the Carnegie Unit in the Foundation's 1934 annual report. "[N]one recognizes more clearly than the Foundation that these standards have served their purpose... They should give place to more flexible, more individual, more exact and revealing standards of performance as rapidly as these may be achieved."[10] And that was in 1934!

In the late 1990s, Carnegie Foundation President Lee Shulman, nationally recognized advocate for assessing teaching and learning by "outcomes," summarized the problem: "There is nothing simple about measuring the quality of learning. The reason for the robustness of the Carnegie Unit is not that it's the best measure, just that it's much more difficult than folks think to replace it."[11]

Others go further and argue that the empirical validity of Carnegie Units as a predictor of student learning has not been demonstrated. These same critics recognize that Carnegie Units continue to enjoy near universal usage because they are "convenient for academic bookkeeping."

3 Seat Time Academic Credit: What Does It Really Measure?

The evidence and arguments against the Carnegie Unit continued to mount in the new century. In 2003, former Carnegie Senior Scholar Thomas Ehrlich, coeditor of the book, *How the Student Credit Hour Shapes Higher Education*, warned that the Carnegie Unit may be "perpetuating bad habits that get in the way of institutional change in higher education."[12]

The Carnegie Commission on Higher Education and the Carnegie Council on Policy Studies in Higher Education have continued efforts to bring change in the way we advance learning and education. These prestigious organizations have proposed new models such as "learning pavilions" and a move away from time-based options including open university models, electronic delivery systems, and others. New technologies that offer alternative modes of teaching and learning are regularly proposed.

Notwithstanding decades of critics and proposals for much-needed new approaches, higher education policy makers and leaders stubbornly continue to use the credit hour as the currency of higher education. The serious, documented limitations of the credit hour for measuring learning or knowledge and the critical need to better align the education mission of our colleges and universities with the needs of the workplace, economy, and society are ignored by education policy makers. The demands for changing the delivery model, performance evaluation, and measuring system for higher education continue to go unheeded in the face of well-documented and well-reasoned proposals for change.

The convenience factor is, perhaps, the major obstacle. As Lee Schulman said, the credit hour is difficult to replace. However, although difficult to replace or change, it is increasingly clear that the credit-hour accounting system has its own cost, a cost we ignore and refuse to calculate.

One area where our colleges and universities are paying a high price for their refusal to change is in public confidence and support for higher education. A recent study, published by The Public Agenda of The Kresge Foundation, released in September 2016, reveals "public confidence in higher education waning." Americans, they found, are suspicious about the "intentions" of colleges and universities. "Nearly six in ten – 59 percent – say colleges today care mainly about the bottom line, versus 34 percent who say colleges today mainly care about education and their students."[13]

Numerous other studies over the past fifteen years document decreasing public confidence in higher education. A nationwide survey of 10,241 nationally representative Americans, published in 2017, found only 14% of Americans have a great deal of confidence in higher education and one in five US adults has "hardly any confidence in how colleges and universities are run."[14]

This deterioration of confidence in American higher education appears to be accelerating. Just a little over a decade ago a survey conducted by Gross and Simmons (2006) found that 42% of Americans reported "a lot of confidence" in colleges and universities.[15] This deterioration of confidence coincides with declining state support in our public universities and may be a factor in legislative decisions to cut subsidies to higher education. Indeed, this loss of confidence is extracting a high price from our colleges and universities, a price they can ill-afford.

Are our colleges and universities, particularly those in the public sector, sustainable in the face of the continuing loss of the public's confidence? This loss of public confidence in higher education makes the task of state legislatures easier when it comes to reducing state subsidies to our public colleges and universities. The argument here is that a new currency or metric for higher education, based on outcome measures of learning and knowledge more aligned with the needs of the workplace, economy, and society, is badly needed and long overdue. New metrics that actually measure knowledge or competency, if adopted, could be the catalyst for reform and the foundation for increased public confidence in higher education.

It may be disingenuous to argue that we have some of the brightest minds in the world on our university campuses and that we can and should figure out how to measure what we do in our institutions of higher education in a manner that has validity, reliability, *and* practicality. Continuing to use the Carnegie credit and refusing to pursue more valid and reliable measures of learning and knowledge undermine the credibility of academic degrees as well as the institutions that award them.

The question from education policy makers is, what are the alternatives and potential options to time-based credit? This is not a new question; alternatives and options have been proposed. Many of them have been in the scholarly discourse and literature for a half century or longer; others are more recent reflecting advances in new technologies.

The Carnegie Foundation for the Advancement of Learning is helping to lead this conversation and generate support for needed change. Among the alternatives they recognize and discuss are (1) assessment of prior learning, (2) direct assessment, (3) competency-based programs, and (4) various hybrids for online learning, distance learning, MOOCs and technology-based modalities. Each of these alternatives is supported by a vast literature documenting their respective strengths and weaknesses.

Large-scale alternatives and options have also been discussed and, in some nations, launched into the policy arena. These include Bologna Process and Degree Qualifications Frameworks. It also includes Tuning, a variation of the Bologna Process and Degree Qualifications Framework more attuned to the American system of higher education.

The European Model: The Bologna Process

Named after the city of Bologna, Italy where in 1999 Europe's education ministers agreed to "harmonize" their national higher education systems through common "reference points," the Bologna Process seeks to put in place a "transparent" mechanism that will recognize the work of a course or the substance of a college degree in terms of "outcomes."

The well-respected publication, *Inside Higher Ed*, describes the Bologna Process as a "Wake Up Call for American Higher Ed." They write that "News analysis of Europe's 'Bologna' movement suggests that colleges in the United States could soon face substantial pressure to better define what their own degrees and credits mean." They cite the extensive and thorough work of Clifford Adelman, higher education policy analyst with the Institute of Higher Education Policy, who argues that "all of higher education in the United States needs to start paying attention to Bologna and adopting some of its features…American higher education risks being passed by."[16] A decade later, the gap, pressure, and need are even greater. Resistance to change, particularly change in the interest of students, has become the hallmark of American higher education.

The Bologna Process has attracted growing attention in the USA as the concerns and criticisms of the "seat time" semester credit hour have increased. One example is the recent comprehensive work by Paul Gaston. Gaston presents the need for an American version of the Bologna Process that retains the strengths of our nation's higher education but that captures the reforms of Bologna that give greater definition to degrees and is "…more germane to the needs and opportunities of the United States."[17]

The Bologna Process offers American higher education an option that, properly modified, will not only address most of the weaknesses, concerns, and criticisms of the semester credit-hour accounting method but would, if adopted, keep American higher education better connected and aligned with the systems of Europe and the other approximately 50 nations of the world that have adopted the Bologna Process.

Another viable option to the semester credit hour is a variation on the Bologna Process, i.e., the Degree Qualifications Framework or Profile (DQP). To its credit, the Lumina Foundation is taking a leadership role in bringing, more clearly and effectively than ever before, the DQP to the American higher education audience and seeks "to set a new direction for U.S. higher education…".[18]

The DQP describes what a student and graduate should know, be able to do, and presents outcomes for each of degree level. The central difference from the semester credit hour is DQP provides a qualitative set of learning outcomes in lieu of traditional quantitive measures such as number of credit hours and grade point averages for awarding degrees. Further, DQP, as described in the Lumina Foundation Report, seeks to organize learning outcomes for the degrees in five "broad interrelated categories," i.e., (1) specialized knowledge, (2) broad, integrative knowledge, (3) intellectual skills, (4) applied and collaborative learning, and (5) civic and global learning.[19]

Jamie Merisotis, President and CEO of the Lumina Foundation, presents the case for moving away from our current time-based credit

3 Seat Time Academic Credit: What Does It Really Measure?   37

system that leads to a degree. Describing the requirements of the twenty-first century, he argues that "students don't need just credentials. What they need—and what our global economy and democratic society increasingly demand—is the learning those credentials signify, the highly developed knowledge and skills that postsecondary education provides." The centerpiece of Merisotis's argument and the thesis of this chapter is "…it's not enough simply to count credentials; the credentials *themselves* must count."[20]

There are signs that this message is starting to register with some American colleges and universities. The Lumina Foundation Report cites more than 400 institutions that have voluntarily engaged in various projects to strengthen student learning. The challenge to American colleges and universities and all those engaged in higher education is to change the paradigm from seat time to learning outcomes as the path to a degree.

A part of the same effort is the Tuning USA initiative. The Tuning initiative is working to develop "field specific reference points that describe a pathway to the students' credential." Faculty groups organized by state education systems are consulting with employers, industries, faculty outside the field as well as students and former students to find consensus on needed or required field-based learning outcomes. Faculty from multiple institutions are encouraged to work with each other to define and agree on those benchmarks for the various stages of progress toward the degree. The objective is to foster active learning that will enable students to demonstrate competencies and proficiencies.[21]

All three of the options described above—The Bologna Process, Degree Qualifications Profile and the Tuning USA initiative—bring a needed new perspective on how to define and measure learning outcomes that lead to a university degree. These options stress active learning, knowledge, and competencies, not seat time credit, as the path to a degree. The new American higher education paradigm must take this, or similar path if it is to meet the needs of the twenty-first-century workforce, marketplace, and global standards that are rapidly outpacing time-based credit and degrees.

Where does the responsibility rest for reform? One of the strengths of the American system of higher education is the autonomy of individual institutions. It is also one of its weaknesses when it comes to bringing change to the system as a whole. Notwithstanding the structural weaknesses of the system, a change in the paradigm is required if the American higher education system is to regain and retain its leadership among the nations or even maintain its current status.

Our colleges and universities are accountable in varying degrees to those who provide the funding and those who award accreditation. For public universities, partial funding comes from the states. Likewise, regional accreditation bodies have significant leverage and influence over our institutions of higher education. These two entities, with the authority they have over our institutions, could be starting points for bringing about change.

In addition to the power of the states and the authority of accreditation bodies, individual institutions must also play a role. Boards of trustees will need to be informed and motivated to gain an understanding of the nature of the current academic credit system. Boards must understand that the semester credit hour does not measure learning or knowledge; they must also understand the need for measures of institutional performance that are tied to the mission. Trustees have a key leadership role in bringing about these important changes.

College and university presidents are on the front lines when it comes to change and they, too, have a significant leadership role to play. Unfortunately, it may be more than we can hope for to expect college and university presidents to play such a role. Most find themselves defending the status quo and keeping others from rocking the academic boat. However, presidents should know that their boards expect them to help lead the change that must come.

Bringing about change to the whole system, particularly a fundamental change to the economic infrastructure, will be difficult and require some time. But, the process has begun and the pressure for change will only increase.

Conclusion

The Carnegie Unit was devised and proposed as a tool to help schools and colleges define the nature of their institutions and find a common standard that allowed colleges to agree on the criterion for a baccalaureate degree. Within a relatively short time, the Carnegie Unit also became the measure for a whole host of other education functions, not because it had some intrinsic quality that, with validity and reliability, operationalized those many functions but because of its simplicity, ease of use, and widespread willingness on the part of institutions to adopt and use the measure. The Carnegie Unit soon evolved into the semester credit hour which, for students, became the currency they were able to bank over a four- or five-year period—or longer—that could be cashed in for a baccalaureate degree.

The role played by the Carnegie Unit was instrumental in helping the nation to rapidly develop one of the best, if not the best, system of higher education in the world. The Unit, a quick and easy, time-based metric, has served as a surrogate, spurious as it is, for learning and knowledge for more than a century. And, it seemed to work notwithstanding the well-known weaknesses of the measure. But the twenty-first century is different: Change has become the new constant and new normal. The growth of science and technology and the rise of the knowledge economy in the USA and other nations now require a more mature, valid and reliable measure of learning, knowledge, and competence.

American higher education has, unfortunately, lagged behind the rapid expansion of knowledge and its application to the growing challenges and opportunities lying before us in the twenty-first century. Some argue, correctly, that the manner in which our colleges and universities measure their productivity and performance has been a "drag" on the nation's economy and an obstacle to the preparation and demands of the workforce required for the full development of our knowledge economy.

New approaches are being developed for measuring more accurately and appropriately the many functions that our system of higher education requires. It is now time, still early in the twenty-first century, to take this issue seriously and adopt, or at least begin experimenting with, new models and measures of learning and knowledge that are more closely aligned with the needs and opportunities in our workforce and economy as well as the higher education systems in Europe and many other parts of the world.

But the question must be asked: Are we too far in, too entrenched in the semester credit hour to change without sacrificing important elements of our higher education system that contributed to its success and even its greatness? Are we locked into a system that cannot be fundamentally changed, only tweaked on its margins? Are we not capable of making the much-needed changes without sacrificing the good?

Taken alone, as if the serious limitations of the semester credit hour were the only crack in the paradigm, their weaknesses and concerns would not, perhaps, be so concerning. But when added to the mix of other cracks, like drug interaction, it can and may well be very serious, even potentially fatal. When the value of a nation's currency is eroded or undermined, the nation's economy plunges into crisis. The semester credit hour is the currency of higher education. It is incumbent on the leaders of higher education to ensure the value, credibility, and validity of its currency.

References

1. John Harris, *Brief History of American Academic Credit System: A Recipe for Incoherence in Student Learning* (Samford University, September 2002).
2. Ibid.
3. Ibid.
4. Elena Silva, Taylor White, and Thomas Toch, *The Carnegie Unit: A Century-Old Standard in a Changing Education Landscape* (Carnegie Foundation for the Advancement of Teaching, 2015).
5. Ibid., p. 9.
6. John Harris, p. 4.
7. Elena Silva et al., pp. 28–29.
8. Ibid.
9. Ibid.
10. Ibid.
11. Ibid.
12. Jane V. Wellman and Thomas Ehrlich (eds.), *How the Student Credit Hour Shapes Higher Education: The Tie That Binds*, New Directions for Higher Education, Number 122 (Jossey-Bass, Single Issue Higher Education Summer 2003).

13. Public Agenda, *New Survey Suggests Public Confidence in Higher Education Waning* (The Kresge Foundation, September 13, 2016).
14. David R. Johnson and Jared L. Peifer, "How Public Confidence in Higher Education Varies by Social Context," *The Journal of Higher Education* (Volume 88, Issue 4, 2017).
15. Ibid.
16. "Wake-Up Call for American Higher Education," *Inside Higher Ed* (May 21, 2008).
17. Paul L. Gaston, *The Challenge of Bologna: What the United States Higher Education Has to Learn from Europe and Why It Matters* (Sterling, VA: Stylus, 2010).
18. "Degree Qualifications Profile," *Lumina Foundation* (October 1, 2014).
19. Ibid.
20. Ibid.
21. Ibid., Appendix B, p. 33.

4

Tenure: Lifetime Employment in a Fast-Changing World

The Tenure Debate

The history of the "tenure debate" in the USA is a history of periods of quietude followed by periods of intense discussion and heated public discord. It is a history that includes periods when scholars conducted detached, objective analyses of the various issues surrounding tenure as well as periods when debate was fueled largely by emotional and often self-serving arguments. The history of the debate has strong proponents and advocates for tenure as well as equally strong antagonists and critics. The debate has gone through periods when the discourse was generally limited to small groups of education policy makers as well as periods when the discourse spilled over into the public arena and popular press.

The tenure debate continues today. There are those who argue that it is tenure that has given American higher education its strength and leadership among nations. There are those who rationalize their support for tenure on the basis of the cost of eliminating it and the higher salaries that would have to be paid to attract faculty to non-tenuring colleges and universities. And, there are those who continue to argue that academic freedom requires the protection that only tenure can provide.

Critics of tenure point to the basic unfairness of protected careers with guaranteed lifetime employment in positions whose salaries are paid for by students and taxpayers. They challenge the stated purpose of tenure as being the only effective way of ensuring academic freedom and object to the rigidity tenure imposes on the ability of university administrations to manage resources and to shift faculty assets when enrollment patterns shift. Some critics have gone so far as to claim that tenure and its companion, the Ph.D., "have inflicted what may turn out to be fatal wounds on higher education."[1]

I've been reviewed and approved for tenure in six universities over a career that spans nearly 50 years. I valued and deeply appreciated the sense of professional approval and job security I felt when that decision was passed down from the president, provost, or dean. Over this same period, I've been directly or indirectly involved and often made the final recommendation or decision on tenure for many faculty candidates. I've spent countless weekends reading the voluminous files that work their way up the administrative chain that are assembled to document the stature and worthiness of candidates for this coveted status.

In my experience at several universities, 90-plus percent of the candidates for tenure received a positive nod and joined the ranks of those with lifetime appointments. It was a very rare occasion when a fellow faculty member failed to receive a positive tenure decision. I can remember only a few such instances.

The major voice and organizational support for academic tenure in the USA is the American Association of University Professors (AAUP). For more than a century, AAUP has been responsible for "developing standards to guide higher education in service of the common good."[2] Within a year of its founding in 1914, AAUP had formulated its first policy statement on tenure, i.e., *1915 Declaration of Principle*. A decade later, AAUP called a conference to review their tenure policy for the purpose of agreeing on "a shorter statement of principles." The updated version was called the *1925 Conference Statement on Academic Freedom and Tenure*.

The concept of tenure that currently serves as the policy framework for American colleges and universities was formulated in 1940 by AAUP in collaboration with the Association of American Colleges and

Universities (AAC&U), i.e., *Statement of Principles on Academic Freedom and Tenure*. The 1940 *Statement* is a fairly brief document that defines and describes academic freedom and tenure. It describes tenure as

> ...a means to certain ends; specifically: (1) freedom of teaching and research and of extramural activities, and (2) a sufficient degree of economic security to make the profession attractive to men and women of ability. Freedom and economic security, hence, tenure, are indispensable to the success of an institution in fulfilling its obligations to its students and to society.[3]

The rationale and major argument for the promulgation of this policy are that college and university faculty "cannot properly fulfill their core responsibilities to advance and transmit knowledge" if they can lose their jobs because of their speech and research publications.

Clearly, tenure has been, and continues to be, a controversial topic—highly controversial in some circles—even when it is not in the headlines of the nation's major newspapers. It is true that the role played by tenure in the nation's colleges and universities is changing. The number and scope of tenure-granting institutions are slowly shrinking as well as the number of tenure and tenure-track positions within colleges and universities. For some, the change is threatening, taking place much too fast and needs to be reversed; for others, the change is occurring at a "snails pace" and far too slowly to address the larger concerns about declining public support for higher education, generally. The tenure debate is nearly a standoff with no major breakthroughs coming from either camp; but there is some change.

The National Center for Education Statistics maintains a database that chronicles historic and current data on the nation's institutions as well as faculty characteristics in the nation's colleges and universities, including data on tenure. Their data show the percent of institutions with tenure systems has been gradually declining. In 1993–1994, for example, 62.6% of all institutions of higher education reported having tenure; this dropped to 55% in 1999–2000 and again to 49.5% in 2007–2008. Today, fewer than half of all institutions of higher education in the USA offer tenure or tenure-track faculty positions.[4]

While several types of colleges and universities witnessed declining percentages that offered tenure, public 4-year institutions remained fairly constant at 90% or more. Nearly 100% of doctoral degree-granting public universities continue to provide tenure-track appointments. At the other end of the spectrum, private for-profit institutions report that only 1.5% offer tenured positions and that percentage has been declining from a high of 7% a few decades ago.

Fifteen years into the twenty-first century, there were approximately 1.6 million professors in American colleges and universities; up from 932,000 in 1995, this represents a 66% increase in twenty years. During the same period, the number of full-time faculty grew from 551,000 to 807,000, or 47%. Part-time faculty, however, increased by 95%, 381,000–784,000, during this twenty-year period. Slightly more than half of university faculty, 52%, are full time with the remaining 48% serving in part-time positions.

One of the more subtle but important changes taking place among the nation's faculty is the declining number and proportion of tenured faculty in relation to other classes of faculty. For example, in the mid-1970s, tenured faculty constituted the largest class of college and university faculty, i.e., approximately 30%. The number of full-time tenured positions has fallen fairly consistently over the past 40+ years; likewise, the number of tenure-track positions has dropped by half during this same period.

An important conversation underway today is the changing nature of the academic workforce, principally, the growth in the number and percentage of part time and adjunct faculty, or contingent faculty. These positions are described differently at different institutions, e.g., non-tenure track, limited term, fixed term, or contract positions and carry different titles such as lecturer, instructor, or even visiting professor. Closely related is the decreasing size and proportion of "regular" tenure and tenure-track faculty. For many full-time faculty, faculty organizations, and some higher education associations, these changes in the academic workforce are viewed as serious challenges to institutional quality standards, the academic professions and even academic freedom.

The stated purpose of and major argument in favor of tenure is to ensure the principle and practice of academic freedom, i.e., the freedom to hold, examine, and discuss different points of view understanding that some may not be politically popular or politically acceptable. Accordingly, free inquiry, free expression, and open dissent are viewed as critically important for the advancement of knowledge, critical thinking, and student learning. If we accept this premise—and most of us in the academy do—it is critically important to have policies and practices in place to protect academic freedom. Many in the academy argue that tenure and tenure alone can serve that purpose. Clearly, however, that is not the case.

Academic freedom is absolutely essential for the academy and to the mission of higher education. Academic freedom forms the intellectual environment required for the open, free expression of ideas, concepts, theories, philosophies, and ideologies. Any infringement of academic freedom would weaken our universities and colleges and the overall quality of education provided by our system of higher education. The question, however, is this: Is a tenured "life-time appointment" essential for the protection and assurance of academic freedom? Phrased another way: Are lifetime appointments a cost-effective way or, as argued by some, the only effective way to guarantee academic freedom?

Economics of Tenure

There is little disagreement that the economics of tenure are a relevant aspect of the "tenure debate." Roger G. Baldwin and Jay L. Chorister, in their provocative essay, "What Happened to the Tenure Track"[5] try to pinpoint why tenure-track faculty appointments have declined in use. Going from the well-documented proposition that there is "no one single, simple explanation" for this trend, they cite three key factors, i.e., economics, flexibility, and access to needed resources. Tenure, they state, is "a costly proposition for colleges and universities." A tenured faculty member can easily serve forty years or longer. Normal annual or periodic salary increments combined with promotions through the academic ranks increase personnel costs to colleges and universities with no practical mechanism for limiting these costs. Surveys of college professors in recent years indicate that 60% or more plan to work past the age of 70.

There are, undoubtedly, many such lengthy tenures; they can be found on nearly every college or university campus. I know faculty members—friends of mine—who are well into their 80s. I met one of these colleagues recently in a favorite campus cafe and he indicated he had no plans to retire…ever. He is in his upper 80s. He jokingly told me "They will have to carry me out of here with my boots on." The collective and cumulative financial impact of the aging faculty and increasing length of their careers has become a large and difficult fiscal challenge. Protected by tenure and law, there are few options for colleges and universities for dealing with this challenge. However, these options should be identified and employed, when needed, in the interest of students and the institutions. Institutions should not be forced by law or policy to make such long-term financial commitments, essentially encumbering multi-million-dollar obligations for each tenured position. It is a non-sustainable practice that works against the fiscal health and viability of our colleges and universities. Most of all, it works against the interests of students.

Charles T. Clotfelter performed a quick "back-of-the-envelope" calculation of the projected cost incurred by a university tenure decision. Here is what he finds:

> For a thirty-two-year old freshly tenured associate professor with a $70,000 salary,…the university faces an expected obligation on the order of $2.7 million in present value terms, assuming he retires at age seventy. If he retires at seventy-five, the expected obligation is $3.0 million.[6]

If this professor decides to continue teaching into his mid-80s like my octogenarian colleagues, just add another million dollars to the tab. And, as Clotfelter notes, these are only the payroll costs and do not include other support costs normally associated with faculty which may include health-care benefits, shared secretarial assistance, travel funds for conferences, office space and maintenance, graduate assistants, etc.

Economists are quick to point out that tenure, as it is presently practiced, also prevents resource reallocations that could help achieve greater efficiencies, greater benefits to students and stronger institutional impacts. Tenured faculty members, for example, housed in departments that may be undergoing decreases in majors, student enrollments, and semester credit hours, may be preventing the reassignment of the needed personnel lines to departments experiencing growth and shortage of faculty. Robert W. McGee and Walter E. Block, in their essay, "Academic Tenure: An Economic Critique," are less diplomatic than some when they write, "Universities must wait for the [tenured] faculty in overstaffed departments to retire or die before resources can be reallocated."[7]

Institutional flexibility is increasingly important to colleges and universities as state funding and subsidies continue to decline as a portion of the total budget and in real dollars. For a decade or longer in many states, presidents and boards of trustees have been under growing pressures to "do more with less." The ability to move assets to achieve maximum productivity and positive outcomes is a must; the ability to eliminate or reduce expenditures in underproducing departments or colleges is essential to meet the growing fiscal challenges confronting our institutions. Tenure constitutes a formidable barrier to institutional flexibility.

Recent studies show the share of faculty, age 65 and older teaching full time at American colleges and universities, nearly doubled between 2000 and 2010. College professors are now among the oldest Americans in the workforce.[8]

Not only are some of these professors occupying positions that may be more efficiently and effectively used in different departments or colleges, the salaries received by senior professors with thirty or forty years of service and promotions to senior ranks are likely twice as much as salaries paid to junior faculty and new hires. Faculty cite job satisfaction, tenure-secured job protection, and concern about their retirement finances as reasons for continuing in their professorial roles. And while their knowledge and experience bring value to their students, departments, and colleges, the higher salaries of senior professors in an era of rising expenses, shrinking state subsidies and endowments—doing more with less—has led many universities to adopt "buyout" policies that provide financial incentives to senior faculty members to retire.

The budgets have become so tight that a growing number of these institutions are targeting buyouts to ever younger faculty, i.e., those with twenty or twenty-five years of service who may be in their late 50s or 60s.

Jonathan R. Cole, among others, has argued that this situation, created by the elimination of mandatory retirement for tenured faculty members in 1993, needs to be revisited and rethought for the benefit of universities and students. "Congress" he argues, "ought to set a mandatory retirement age for faculty members at some age, perhaps seventy-five,..."[9] Cole goes on to add, however, that such faculty "should have many of the same privileges that they held while full-time faculty members."

This is one of those situations that demand a more flexible, creative approach. Would it not be prudent, for example, for tenure-granting colleges and universities to avoid the increasing number of multi-million-dollar encumbrances for senior, tenured faculty like the ones described above, by limiting the *tenure* status to a defined number of years or specific age, e.g., 65 or 70? If the university does not need the faculty personnel line for another department or other budget exigencies, the funding could be pooled to support senior faculty members who could continue teaching without tenure for as long as resources were available and the expertise or discipline of the faculty member was in demand.

There is also a case for mandatory retirement for university faculty, i.e., status quo ante. Numerous professions have such mandated retirement, e.g., pilots, air traffic controllers, federal law enforcement officers, park rangers, and even the judiciary in a growing number of states. In the case of college and university faculty, the policy would not necessarily call for full "mandatory retirement" but rather a time-limited tenure policy that would end at a specified age or at the end of a defined period.

Clearly, tenure is much more than just securing academic freedom. Today, more than ever, the awarding of tenure and tenure policies, in general, need to take into account the economics of such decisions and their long-term impact on the fiscal health of the institution and cost implications for students. How, for example, does tenure and the protections of tenure for senior faculty drive college and university costs? How does tenure impact the capability of institutions to reallocate resources as student interests and demands change over time? These and related questions should be raised by trustees keeping in mind their fiduciary responsibilities and the impact of their decisions today on the future and long-term sustainability of their colleges and universities.

McGee and Block take the tenure economics argument a giant step further: They argue that awarding a status to faculty that protects them from those who pay their salaries—taxpayers, students, and their families—is problematic and wrong. They write:

> …taxpayers and consumers of education must often support the careers of academics of whom they disagree. In effect, those who advocate tenure on the grounds of academic freedom claim that academics have a right to the hard-earned dollars of others even if those who earn the dollars do not support the academics' views. In the view of tenure advocates, academic freedom justifies forcing others to support an academic's views with their cash.[10]

This point of view—extreme by current standards—may be more widely held than we suspect. While I have not personally heard any direct criticism levied at a particular professor for their politics or philosophy, I have heard some of my business and other friends take the position that "these liberal professors—protected by tenure—advocate views and values contrary to mine and I'm paying their salaries with my tax dollars and daughter's tuition." It is this perspective, held by some, that causes concern. It is this public opinion—sometimes loudly expressed—that gives quiet license to state legislatures to continue whittling away at the subsidies and support for higher education.

The Half-Life of Knowledge

> The half-life of knowledge or half-life of facts is the amount of time that has to elapse before half of the knowledge or facts in a particular area is superseded or shown to be untrue.[11]

This proposition is based on the work of Samuel Arbesman, author of *The Half-Life of Facts: Why Everything We Know Has an Expiration Date*. A senior scholar at the Kaufmann Foundation and an expert in scientometrics, Arbesman conducts studies on how facts are "made and remade in the modern world." And since fact-making is speeding up, he and others worry that "most of us don't keep up to date and base our decisions on facts we dimly remember from school and university classes that turn out to be wrong."[12]

The implications of the "half-life" theory of knowledge and facts for higher education could be quite profound. Anyone who has taught for any length of time in a science or social science discipline, not to mention all the other fields of knowledge, knows the pressure of staying "current." The sheer volume of conference proceedings, journals, and books produced every year—or even every month—defies our best efforts to stay up with the latest research findings and growing bodies of knowledge even in the very narrow fields of our specializations.

Ron Bailey, in his review of Abresman's work, writes that scientific knowledge is growing by a factor of ten every 50 years. This means that half of what scientists may have known about a particular subject will be wrong or obsolete in 45 years. And, half-lives keep getting shorter. The knowledge base of an engineering degree went from a half-life of 35 years in the 1930s to about 10 years in the 1960s. The current half-life of the knowledge base of psychology is estimated to be about five years.

Aside from the economics of tenure and the financial obligations to maintain this protected status—which should *not* be the sole criteria for a position on the question of tenure—there is the greater issue of the increasingly rapid growth of knowledge. With this growth of knowledge comes the need for universities to constantly strive to ensure that teaching, research, and service performed by faculty reflect the current or latest knowledge available in their respective fields of inquiry. Faculty trained in a particular field, however, often carry their views forward, sometimes for decades, despite significant changes that may have occurred in that field. Outdated perspectives, methods, theories, and philosophies are expressed far too often in lectures, classroom discussions, syllabi, and teaching materials.

In this age of rapid social change, accelerating advances in technologies, increasing globalization of education, new theories, and perspectives in nearly every field of inquiry and an explosion of knowledge and methods for communicating this knowledge, it is of the greatest importance that universities—particularly comprehensive research institutions—maintain faculties that are fully current with the *latest* research and developments in their respective fields. Tenure policies, as they are currently applied, are a major reason universities often fail that test.

Every university with which I've been associated has had its share of tenured faculty members who were "hanging on" despite the obsolescence of their lectures, the datedness of their case studies, lack of intellectual curiosity and physical and mental energy required by today's professoriate. Universities owe it to their students and those who underwrite the cost of public higher education, including the support of tenure, that the content of our courses and pedagogy are the latest and best information and knowledge relevant to the course.

Post-Tenure Review

The discussions, debates, public criticism, legislative opposition, and concerns of a sizable number of university trustees about the function, role, and impact of tenure began to take their toll in the 1980s. Calls for greater accountability in the form of post-tenure reviews were beginning to be heard by university presidents, provosts, faculty senates, and associations supporting higher education in the USA. Most campuses, with support from AAUP, resisted these calls for greater accountability. Cathy A. Trower describes the changing 1980s landscape of tenure in the following:

> The AAUP initially denounced post-tenure review in 1983 as a threat to academic freedom and tenure; however, during the 1990s, its position changed. In its report "Post-Tenure Review: An AAUP Response" (1998) the association set "minimum standards for good practice if a formal system of post-tenure review is established."[13]

The ten AAUP standards for post-tenure review stressed the centrality of academic freedom and the need to protect it "at all costs." Faculty should have the responsibility for developing and conducting these reviews and have administrative assurance that such reviews were "not a pretense for revisiting the tenure decision." The standards called for constructing post-tenure reviews in a "developmental" manner and that meritorious performance be rewarded. The review processes and outcomes were to be kept confidential and any needed "developmental plan" should be designed by the faculty member under review and the administration.

In June, 1999, AAUP issued the following position statement further clarifying its policy on post-tenure review:

> Post-tenure review ought to be aimed not at accountability, but at faculty development. Post-tenure review must be developed and carried out by faculty. Post-tenure review must not be a reevaluation of tenure, nor may it be used to shift the burden of proof from an institution's administration (to show cause for dismissal) to the individual faculty member (to show cause why he or she should be retained). Post-tenure review must be conducted according to standards that protect academic freedom and the quality of education.[14]

Read by anyone outside the academy or not a part of the academic culture, the AAUP standards and policy positions, as well as their adoption by the majority of the nation's colleges and universities, would appear foreign, if not contrary, to the nation's workforce norms and ethics. Where is the "accountability?" How can the public and their representatives in state legislatures support "their colleges and universities" when accountability for the performance of tenured faculty is ambiguous or non-existent. For some, the idea of tenure that gives largely unaccountable lifetime jobs to anyone seems unlike the American work ethic.

Cost-Benefit of Tenure

How should one weigh the value of tenure? Would a "cost-benefit" analysis be worth the time and effort? What does a college or university gain from embracing tenure as their way of ensuring academic freedom?

4 Tenure: Lifetime Employment in a Fast-Changing World

What are the costs and benefits of tenure to students? And, what are the costs and benefits to those who support higher education with their tax dollars and tuition? Are there ways to ensure academic freedom outside of tenure? Are there ways of accruing the benefits of tenure without guaranteed lifetime appointments and the associated costs?

The answers to these and scores of related questions that have been posed for nearly a century differ depending on who's asking and who's answering. It is a value-laden issue with strong and deep vested interests on both sides.

McGee and Block try to answer the question: Is tenure cost-effective? They argue that two teaching positions, paying the same salary and every thing else being equal with the exception that one comes with tenure and the other without tenure, because most people are risk-averse, the one with tenure would be selected over the one without. Eliminating tenure at a university where it exists would be "equivalent to reducing professors' salaries. Therefore, the possession of tenure has some value." And, because it has value, faculty who have tenure, or are hired to a tenure-track position, "will work for less money than professors who cannot hope to receive a guarantee of lifetime employment."[15]

Tenure-granting universities do not have to pay tenured or tenure-track faculty the same salaries as those who work without tenure and the economic security that comes with tenure. From a university perspective, this has the appearance of a financial benefit, albeit a benefit for a limited period of time. However, McGee and Block argue that while tenure appears to be a fiscal benefit to colleges and universities because of the lower salaries they can offer, the cost-effectiveness argument in support of tenure is "unpersuasive." If the cost-effective argument was valid, "all employers would reduce labor costs by guaranteeing lifetime employment." But education is the only sector where tenure is practiced to any degree. Reason: "…lifetime employment guarantees reduce flexibility" and because markets, by their nature change, market-dependent businesses must be able to retain the flexibility to adapt to these changes.[16]

The "cost" of tenure to colleges and universities is in the lack of flexibility it brings to personnel costs. Tenure-granting colleges and universities are not able to eliminate faculty positions filled by a tenured professor even when student demand for the courses and expertise of that professor no longer justify its continuation. A market-dependent business—unprotected by government, accrediting bodies, and other insulators—would not be sustainable with an inflexible personnel policy that prevented firings, layoffs, or reassignment.

McGee and Block conclude their analysis of the cost-benefit analysis of tenure with the following:

> Although tenure may allow universities to hire faculty at lower salaries, total salary costs may be higher under a tenure system because universities will be forced to hire more faculty to teach popular disciplines and will not be able to fire unneeded faculty who teach unpopular subjects.[17]

Richard Chait calls attention to other not-so-visible costs of tenure. As one of the nation's leading authorities on tenure, Chait points out that "tenure creates excessive social, as well as individual, costs because unproductive tenured faculty limit opportunities for new faculty and programmatic innovation."[18] In addition to common sense arguments as well as economic analyses, surveys of faculty—those with the most to gain from tenure—reveal sizable proportions who see and understand the broader costs of the tenure system. Chait cites a Carnegie Foundation (1989) study that found nearly 4 out of 10 faculty under age 39 agreed that "abolition of tenure would, on the whole, improve the quality of American higher education." Nearly 3 out of 10 faculty of all ages agreed that abolishing tenure would improve higher education.

A more recent study of faculty opinions on tenure, conducted by the UCLA Higher Education Research Institute, revealed that 38% of faculty (35% for male faculty and 46% for female faculty) agreed that "tenure is an outmoded concept."[19]

In the last half century, the tenure debate has produced an encyclopedia of studies, countless research papers, hundreds of journal articles, uncountable opinion pieces, and scores of books, and monographs on the topic. Few, if any, argue against the critical importance of academic freedom for the professoriate; what is argued is the view that tenure is the only sure way of ensuring academic freedom. Nothing, for example, prevents colleges and universities from embracing academic freedom in their Missions, Values Statements, and By-laws or inclusion of iron-clad agreements in faculty union contracts or even in individual faculty contracts.

Lifetime job security to ensure academic freedom is, to be very clear, a costly scam that continues to be perpetrated by AAUP, their constituents and members. Tenure that means lifetime job security, irrespective of the needs of students and the costs imposed on universities, students, and the state, is an unaffordable anachronism that must be given a "sunset" clause if our system of public higher education is to survive the mounting challenges of the market, technology, and this new era.

Conclusions

We are at a point in time when a full, open, honest national discussion of the costs and benefits of tenure, as a way of ensuring academic freedom, should be launched: There are multiple methods for ensuring and protecting academic freedom. Promising lifetime employment may be one of the least favorable, most costly methods for achieving this important objective.

Tenure policies, as they are currently applied in most universities, are one of the deepest "cracks" in America's higher education paradigm. These policies weaken the capacity of colleges and universities to ensure the latest and best in their mission to develop and transfer knowledge to new generations of students. Methods other than lifetime appointments are readily available for ensuring that academic freedom prevails on every campus, for every professor, and those methods need to become the substance of a national conversation in the higher education community.

Acknowledgements Much of the information and material presented in this chapter has greatly benefitted from the scholarship and leadership of Richard P. Chait. His work in this area has been of enormous benefit to scholars, colleges and universities as well as higher education, generally. Of particular value has been Chait's edited volume, *The Questions of Tenure*, Harvard University Press, 2002.

References

1. Page Smith, *Killing the Spirit* (New York: Viking Penguin, 1990), 114.
2. AAUP Website.
3. AAUP, *Statement of Principles on Academic Freedom and Tenure, 1940.*
4. Digest of Education Statistics, *Percent of Full-Time Instructional Faculty with Tenure...Selected Years, 1993–94 Through 2009–10* (US Department of Education, National Center for Education Statistics, September 2010).
5. Roger G. Baldwin and Jay L. Chorister, "What Happened to the Tenure Track?," in Richard P. Chait (ed.), *The Questions of Tenure* (Cambridge, MA: Harvard University Press, 2002).
6. Charles T. Clotfelter, "Can Faculty Be Induced to Relinquish Tenure?," in Chait (ed.), ibid., pp. 222–223.
7. Robert W. McGee and Walter E. Block, "Academic Tenure: An Economic Critique," *Harvard Journal of Law and Public Policy* (Volume 14: 545–563, reprinted in Walter E. Block, *Labor Economics from a Free Market Perspective* [New Jersey: World Scientific, 2008]), 345–363.
8. *Aging Workforce Series*, TIAA/CREF, 2012.
9. Jonathan R. Cole, *Toward a More Perfect University*, (New York: Public Affairs, Perseus Books Group, 2016), 249.
10. Robert W. McGee and Walter E. Block, ibid., p. 552.
11. Samuel Arbesman, *The Half-Life of Facts: Why Everything We Know Has an Expiration Date* (New York: Penguin Group, 2012).
12. Ibid.
13. Cathy A. Trower, "What Is Current Policy?," in Richard P. Chait, ibid., p. 53.
14. Ibid., pp. 53–54.
15. Robert W. McGee and Walter E. Block, ibid.
16. Ibid.
17. Ibid., p. 550.
18. Richard P. Chait, Why Tenure? Why Now?, in Richard P. Chait, ibid., pp. 6–31.
19. Ernst Benjamin, "Some Implications of Tenure for the Profession and Society," American Association of University Professors quoted from *The Chronicle of Higher Education* (September 13, 1996), 12–15A.

5

Campuses: Overvalued, Underused, and Very Costly

Take a walk across any college or university campus in June, July, or early August, and in most cases, you find the usual hubbub of congested sidewalks, oversubscribed parking lots, and buildings overflowing with students and faculty scrambling shoulder-to-shoulder to make class on time has subsided to a calm, relaxed, vacation-like pace. Some campuses are even quieter if there are no summer offerings or the summer program is a small session, as it is on many campuses, with only a few courses being offered.

The university campus we have known and loved—a place of memories, fun, and full of all kinds of activities as well as learning—may soon take on a very different character as students and faculty increasingly opt for the convenience of on-line study. Add to this the reduced demands for traditional campus classrooms as off-campus experiential education, study abroad, competency-based credit and diplomas become stronger or, perhaps, even the norm. These trends are already underway and no one expects them to do anything but grow stronger.

Until recently, higher education was synonymous with the idea of a campus. College or university was a *place* one went to "get an education" much like stores were places one went to "shop." Who ever thought you could earn a university degree sitting in your own private study, on your patio, at your kitchen table, summer vacation spot, or even the beach. But off-campus degrees are being awarded in ever greater numbers as "on-line" has become the preferred mode of learning for an ever-increasing number of students, even students living on campus. It is conceivable and very likely that much like the on-line shopper, this *new* university student—the on-line student—will become the largest segment of the student market very soon.

Technology and economics have come together to create the most disruptive innovation in higher education in the past hundred years, i.e., the on-line classroom and degree. Digital learning in combination with the high cost of tuition for on-campus degrees is creating major questions about the future of college campuses. Where is higher education to take place in the future? On-campus? On-line? Or, some combination of both? The trends are clear and the data conclusive: On-line higher education will have a major role and very large market share—perhaps the largest—in the very near future. What does that mean for the thousands of campuses and the tens of thousands of buildings and facilities that now dot the nation's landscape and communities in every state?

I recall that the largest number of students enrolled in the on-line courses at the university where I served in the early 2000s was not the non-traditional student, as we intended, locked into a job, location, or situation that prevented enrolling in a campus course. Rather, most of those enrolled in our on-line courses were our own resident students taking the course for convenience or the freedom to avoid a required class scheduled at a time they would rather be doing something other than attending class. These were the early adopters of our on-line courses. The higher education community is still unsure about the nature and size of the on-line student market. It is still growing and changing, and universities are still trying to assess the full implications of this changing student market for their curricula, offerings, and campuses. This unprecedented disruption has created an uncertain future for higher education that has not been resolved.

Campus-Based Higher Education

Many higher education leaders and policy makers remember the shocking prediction from Peter Drucker in 1997 when he said in an interview published by Forbes: "Thirty years from now the big university campuses will be relics. Universities won't survive. It is as large a change as when we first got the printed word." His paradigm-rattling prediction came before the impact of the Internet, global expansion of the World Wide Web and the ubiquitous personal connectivity that can be found in nearly every modern country of the world.

There is nearly a decade remaining in Drucker's prediction and most of our big universities still appear strong. However, this 1997 prediction that few believed would or could happen is now more likely than any thought possible at the time. The strains and pressures on the current higher education paradigm—notwithstanding appearances—are greater than at any time in recent history. Vanderbilt University researcher, Tuan Nguyen, recently wrote "The physical 'brick and mortar' classroom is starting to lose its monopoly as a place of learning... 92% of all distance and online education studies find that distance and online education is at least as effective, if not better, than traditional education."[1] Therein lies the growing competition between on-campus and on-line higher education.

Peter Drucker is no longer alone in his prediction of massive change in American higher education. Former presidents, provosts, and professors are expressing the same concerns, calling attention to the growing problems and the serious challenges to the infrastructure of American higher education. Policy researchers are producing data, analyses, and findings that learning cannot be held hostage to the campus classroom. The catalyst for these changes is rooted in the economics of higher education and rapidly rising cost of tuition and fees that have driven students and their families into decades of debt. It is common knowledge that we must peel back the layers of costs that have been added to the college tuition tab and find ways to cut costs and increase opportunities for learning that meet the needs of the labor market and society.

The tools, technologies, and incentives are in place and positioned for a major, even disruptive change.

One of the largest components of collegiate costs is the construction and maintenance of campus buildings and facilities. College leaders and their boards continue to spend untold billions of dollars annually to add to their campus inventories of buildings and facilities with no deceleration on the horizon. To the contrary, these same college and university leaders, supported by their boards of trustees, are accelerating the expansion of their campuses and facilities. Simultaneous with the continued expansion and upgrading of campuses, the campus-centered business model of public higher education is beginning to look obsolete, even "old school" as students increasingly seek less costly, more convenient modes of higher education. Former president of Princeton University, William Bowen, describing the way universities are spending extravagantly on "shiny graduate centers, libraries and accommodations to attract students," calls it a "cost disease." Others, watching the bond ratings, credit status, and growing debt of universities and their students, call it a "death spiral."[2]

The purpose of this treatise is to bring the most serious challenges to public higher education to the fore and to consider them in the light and context of changing times, changing technologies, and changing economics. Clearly, the growing tab for new buildings, renovations, expanded and upgraded facilities, and deferred maintenance is a very serious challenge—a challenge that few are discussing in the context of all the other changes and challenges impacting public higher education. Displacement of campus-based education by virtual universities and digital communications is taking place without a Plan B for our colleges and universities. In view of the histories of college and university campuses and the changing dynamics of higher education, Jonathan R. Cole argues forcefully and correctly that "...we must rethink the American university campus."[3] Education leaders and state-level higher education policy makers would do well to begin serious discussions and planning for the looming prospects of a post-campus university sometime in the not-too-distant future.

The driving pressure for a new digital paradigm for teaching and learning is not coming from higher education leaders or professors as much as it is from students. Virtual reality, for the newest generations of university students, is reality. It is their world and they are quite comfortable living and learning in this new environment. The idea of a virtual campus or digital university is not strange to students. Such concepts are easily integrated into their ways of thinking about education.

A personal experience helped to bring home this new reality. Several years ago, I was invited to attend the opening of a new library at the University of Texas, San Antonio. The attendees gathered in the lobby where the ribbon was cut and we proceeded to take the elevator to the main floor of the new library. When the elevator door opened, we were all stunned to find nothing in the large room but rows of computer stations. There was not a book in sight. This was the new reality. Today, university students carry their own computer station in their pocket or backpack. They don't even have to visit the library for that.

Today, universities across the nation are heavily engaged in digitizing millions of documents, manuscripts, books, historical photographs, music scores, maps, and other materials. Archival materials from rare and special collections are now readily available in digital form. Entire libraries are being digitized for more efficient storage and greater access. While university libraries remain the intellectual "center" of their campuses, this centrality is increasingly symbolic and less physical.

The High Cost of the University Campus

There are now over 4500 college and university campuses in the USA enrolling 22.4 million students. If you add occupational and vocational training schools, the number of campuses jumps to over 5300. California, with 448 colleges and universities, is home to the nation's largest number of institutions of higher education, 184 of which are two-year schools. Alaska, with 6 colleges and universities, has the smallest number. The total value of the nation's college and university campuses has not been calculated, but there is little doubt that it is well into the trillions of dollars representing one of the nation's largest capital investments. Interestingly and even puzzling, campus leaders and boards of trustees keep adding to the inventory of costly buildings in this period of unprecedented uncertainty. Dodge Data & Analytics, a private company that tracks construction in higher education, reports that colleges and universities spent $11.5 billion in a recent year renovating and constructing 21 million square feet of more new space.[4]

Those who enjoy going on-line and searching for information about the nation's colleges and universities will find no end to their enjoyment. If they are looking for "campuses," there will be any number of subheadings including "the 35 biggest colleges in the U.S.," "the 100 most beautiful college campuses in America," "the best National universities," "the 10 universities with the most undergraduate students," and the list goes on. Great, unparalleled diversity exists among the nation's thousands of college and university campuses. The USA has many of the world's greatest campuses and has served as a model to other nations building their own universities and systems of higher education.

But much of this picture is beginning to change driven by economics and technology. Thousands of these beautiful public college and university campuses have become or are fast becoming financial albatrosses to their host states. State legislatures across the nation are raising serious questions about the cost of their campuses, while university presidents and governing boards struggle with a host of issues related to the future role and function of campuses in the changing higher education environment.

The rising cost of building and maintaining university campuses is now forcing some boards and administrations to look for ways of "reducing their physical footprints." Entire buildings, tired from decades of student use, or seriously out of date, are increasingly taken "off-line" and shuttered with the hope that some wealthy alum or foundation will come along and underwrite the cost of bringing it back into use with the latest bells and whistles of campus technologies and amenities. These buildings even have a name: Presidents and vice presidents for development call them "naming opportunities." Some of these old buildings are being leveled to create more open space or to reclaim the land for some future building when times are better.

Among the many daunting campus-related questions is the issue of student housing. Residence halls, or "dorms" in yesterday's parlance,

5 Campuses: Overvalued, Underused, and Very Costly

built in the 1960s, 1970s, and even 1980s, are no longer attractive to students who just assume they will have the option of living in a suite with separate bedrooms and private showers but, perhaps, sharing a common space for entertaining guests. Most universities have undertaken major renovations of their old-style dorms to bring them up to the new standards for residence halls expected by students and their families. Other universities are reaching out to private developers with proposals and invitations to take over the student residential market and, as an incentive, provide the land with little or no cost on which to build these new residence halls.

The academic calendar, another anachronistic leftover from a previous era, also poses a major concern when it comes to maximizing the use of campus buildings. The "academic year," for all practical purposes, is only three-quarters of a calendar year if you consider the two four-month semesters that make up the "year." Add to that the breaks and holidays in the fall, Christmas and New Years, spring break, and other holidays and the actual number of days most campus building are in full use add up to a little over six months a year. A colleague and former university president commented that the high-cost and low-use patterns found at many college and university campuses "challenges rationality."

The cost and use patterns of traditional college and university campuses, while not quite an anachronism, are among the growing concerns of policy makers and legislatures that fund all these campuses. Projecting the cost of operating and maintaining these campuses—with many of their buildings dating back a half century or more—raise serious questions about the need for and affordability of university campuses in the future.

The university campus is now at the vortex of crosscurrents created by advances in technology and the new economic realities of public higher education. With the attractions of new teaching and learning technologies as well as an understanding of the politics and economics of public higher education at the state level, one does not need a crystal ball to see and to project major changes in the near future. Indeed, the changes already underway are just a few of the precursors of a major paradigm shift in the nation's public higher education.

Campus Use in the Digital Era

What is the future of the American university campus? How will the rapid changes in technology and digitization impact university campuses, the way they provide instruction and organize learning resources? Will colleges and universities adopt these new technologies? Will they seek to leverage the benefits and economies of these technologies for students? If so, how will these changes alter the role and function of university campuses? Or, as former president of University of Michigan, James Duderstadt and his colleagues ask, "Will the university as a physical place continue to hold its relevance?"[5]

James Soto Antony, director of the higher education program at Harvard's graduate school of education, quoted in a timely paper, *It's the End of the University As We Know It*, that colleges asking these questions "do so at their own peril."[6] It appears, with a few notable exceptions, that the vast majority of colleges and universities, their governing board members, and campus leaders are, indeed, afraid to ask such questions but most know they will soon be confronted with demands for answers.

The standard practice at most universities is to address the issues related to their physical campuses through a process called "campus master planning." The master plans that I am familiar with, however, commonly project or propose new buildings and upgrading older facilities often without the benefit of clearly projecting future needs, long-term use patterns and continuing costs for utilities, maintenance, and depreciation. Each administration, including their governing boards, wants to leave their imprint on the campus; for many, the way they choose to leave their imprint is in the form of new buildings and campus expansion.

I've always strongly believed that our institutions of higher education should demonstrate genuine, *proactive* leadership in the advancement of learning and knowledge. Education is *our* business and *our* mission and if not our colleges and universities, who will take a leadership role in advancing learning and knowledge? Sadly, not only is higher education not a proactive leader in its own enterprise, many universities are not even adopting the technologies that have been shown effective nor adapting to current applications of technology to classroom teaching much beyond PowerPoint presentations of lecture notes flashed on 1950s pull-down movie screens.

American colleges and universities have been slow to adopt or even to adapt to the technology changes readily available for teaching and learning. While enrollment and classroom management software is increasingly common on campuses, technology for teaching and learning beyond the PowerPoint is still relatively rare. Former president of Harvard University, Larry Summers, laments that innovation in higher education "hasn't yet been pursued on a scale and with a degree of energy that is commensurate with the real challenge."[7] Change is proceeding on most campuses but at a pace that lags behind business, industry, health, and government.

There is, however, a growing sense that the pressures for change emanating from new cost-effective learning technologies will continue to increase until they simply overpower the deeply embedded and outdated pedagogical traditions found on the nation's university campuses. Even casual observers of academic life and culture see the new paradigm on the horizon or, perhaps more accurately, in "the cloud." When change does come, when the paradigm does shift—as it surely will in the near future—it will alter the very foundation of higher education and the structures and institutions associated with it. The Economist describes it well: "The staid higher education business is about to experience a welcome earthquake."[8]

When MIT recently celebrated its centennial in Cambridge, it used the occasion to look ahead and ask, what's next for this institution? What does the future of education look like at MIT? More generally, what does the future of higher education look like? Anant Agarwal, Professor of Electrical Engineering and Computer Science, predicts the future of education at MIT is digital. "We have come so far in the past five to ten years that it's absolutely unimaginable...And the confluence of cloud computing, social networking, video distribution at scale, game design, artificial intelligence have really brought a whole new level of performance and ability."[9]

Those who see and understand the impact of digitalization on higher education have been sending warning signals urging educators and policy makers to make ready for massive change. In one of the most thoughtful and thorough discussions of this topic, James Duderstadt, President Emeritus of the University of Michigan writes,

> We are on the threshold of a revolution that is making the world's accumulated information and knowledge accessible to individuals everywhere, a technology that will link us together into new communities never before possible or even imaginable. This has breathtaking implications for education, research, and learning and, of course, for our colleges and universities…[10]

The unimaginable, however, is happening. What were futuristic visions a decade ago are today's reality. Discussions, conferences, innovative technologies, and courageous university leaders have created actual examples of virtual, campusless colleges and universities, many of which are found outside the USA, in places like South Korea, Syria, Nigeria, and other countries in Africa, Asia, and the Middle East. These discussions and examples demonstrate the transition from traditional bricks and mortar campus classrooms to cyberspace and classrooms in the cloud. These examples also demonstrate the paradigm shift required by American universities if they plan to tap into the huge underserved student marketplace in the USA and globally.

The attractions of the virtual university are obvious: Time and place cease to be issues for students and the opportunities for cutting the cost of higher education to levels affordable by students in nearly every socioeconomic strata make the new paradigm attractive to a major part of the student marketplace. An additional attraction to this student market is their familiarity with digital communication and satisfaction they take in being in control of their learning. For the nation's colleges and universities, the virtual campus opens the door to students from nearly every country and expands the potential student marketplace many fold.

With the mounting pressures, colleges and universities will soon begin shifting—slowly at first but with increasing speed—from physical to cyber campuses. One finds it very difficult to expect or even envision traditional college and university campuses retaining their share of the student market when alternatives for quality higher education can be had at a fraction of their traditional costs, when classes can be scheduled in a manner that fits one's life and work schedules, when students can be taught by some of the world greatest professors and scholars, and where national borders and distance are no longer obstacles. The technological advances of the digital age and the potential for substantial cost savings are now challenging the value of the traditional campus for delivering a quality education.

Campuses' Dirty Little Secret: Deferred Maintenance

Campuses, it turns out, are second only to personnel costs in most university budgets. Construction, maintenance, cleaning, heating, cooling, power, water, and repairs, not to mention depreciation, and deferred maintenance gobble up tens of millions of dollars annually on most major university campuses. In many states, these funds come in separate state allocations under the heading of Capital Budgets but are, nevertheless, a significant part of the operating costs of higher education and a major driver of ever higher student tuition.

The scope of the problem is daunting and clearly reflected in the situation now faced by California's three systems of higher education, i.e., University of California, California State University, and California Community College systems. The three systems together support 147 campuses and nearly 14,000 buildings. Lee Gardner, writing for the *Chronicle of Higher Education,* describes the campus buildings, many now a half century old or older, as needing upgrading, renovating, or replacement. "The Cal State system alone," writes Gardner, "has a backlog of more than $2 billion in deferred maintenance work" and is increasing by more than $140 million annually. This is just *one* of three systems in a single state.[11]

The full picture and cost of deferred maintenance for California's three systems are several times larger than the Cal State system. However, it is the national picture that demands attention and solutions:

Every state faces the same dilemma. The deferred maintenance picture for university campuses in all 50 states is conservatively estimated to be $50 billion or more. My own state of Ohio here in the Midwest, with its 14 public universities, has a deferred maintenance backlog now approaching $3.0 billion covering everything from antiquated steam systems, plumbing, electrical upgrades, tuck pointing deteriorating brick facilities, roofing, window replacements, and more. The Ohio State University reported nearly $700 million in deferred maintenance in 2016. Some Ohio universities are taking on additional debt to help defray their mounting deferred maintenance costs.

Behind the public facades, Corinthian columns, bell towers, manicured lawns, and new buildings which we so proudly tout and display, the mounting costs for deferred maintenance and campus upkeep continue to grow with no end in sight. And, behind the need for "keeping up appearances," is the strong, almost overwhelming sense of competition with other universities in their efforts to attract students and impress families. New and expanded recreation centers, complete with climbing walls and state-of-the-art exercise technologies, new and expanded stadiums and field houses, simulation centers and laboratories, apartment-style residence halls, multiple swimming pools, and more add to the inventory of campus facilities as well as future costs for utilities, upkeep, and maintenance. Campuses across the nation spent a record $11.5 billion in 2015 building new facilities in the hope of attracting students at a time when enrollments have stabilized or, in some states, are declining. This competition is so fierce that among university leaders, it is commonly referred to as "an arms race."

The deferred maintenance problem is further compounded by decisions to add to the campus building inventory. Each new building or facility adds to the inventory that must be maintained. The maintenance required for these expanding campus facilities creates even greater strains on university resources and adds billions of dollars of debt for which the institutions or someone—most likely students and taxpayers—must pay the interest.

The decision in 2014 by Ohio University to take out a 100-year, $250 million bond to fund deferred maintenance projects is characteristic of what is happening on campuses across the nation.[12] The added cost of 100 years of interest that must be paid becomes someone else's problem. In the meantime, current leaders and governing board members have the satisfaction of addressing some of the deferred maintenance and sprucing up the campus at the expense of future students and constituents.

This period of mounting costs for deferred maintenance comes at a time when state legislatures are demonstrating little sympathy for the plight of their campuses and, in fact, are reducing appropriations in many states. Many in the state houses across the country feel justified backing away from funding deferred maintenance and point to the decisions of university governing boards and their presidents to build "first class luxury facilities" at the same time their huge deferred maintenance costs continue to mount.

Escalating costs for deferred maintenance combined with the added interest on bonds sold to help pay these costs add to the growing total cost of higher education. University officials lament the fact that they seem to lose ground every year and there is nowhere to go for the additional funds but to students. Some universities have added special "capital renewal fees" to student tuition bills to help cover the cost for renovations and improvements. There are few, if any, realistic options.

Deferred maintenance costs for university campuses are a growing challenge and deep concern for public universities and for the states that fund them. When these costs are considered in the context of the aging of the campus and declining use of some buildings, they are even more difficult to justify. And, then, as always, there is the question of who pays? Is this a cost that can be transferred to students or should it remain the responsibility of the states' taxpayers? Or, some combination of both? In the meantime, the tab for deferred maintenance continues to grow.

Conclusion: The Future of the Campus

The old, somewhat humorous quote, "*The future ain't what it used to be*" attributed to Yogi Berra, clearly applies to higher education in the USA and most of the nations of the world. The tectonic plates of the higher education infrastructure are shifting, and none of the movement is larger or stronger than that brought on by the forces of technology combined with the economics of rising costs, steeply rising tuition and mandatory fees. Policy analysts and concerned scholars of higher education who have looked behind the curtains into the inner-workings of our colleges and universities are seeing these disruptive forces—innovations and economics—and recognize the coming changes these forces will bring to our very traditional colleges and universities, indeed, all of higher education.

The warnings have been clear and numerous. Illustrative of these "heads-up" warnings are those from some of our leading institutions and private consulting firms that specialize in higher education. Professor Agarwal of MIT, for example, tells us, "The world is clamoring for something more modular, something that you can do flexibly, something that you do anywhere, anytime, even just in case." He and the MIT Task Force on the Future of Education predict that education in the future will be "diffuse, unbundled, on demand, just in time, and just in case."[13]

Others looking behind the curtain see little evidence that higher education, generally, is ready or willing to change. The college and university campus—buildings, facilities, and physical plant—is just one more example of higher education's faithful, but increasingly irrational, allegiance to the *status quo*. A private firm that works with the higher education community on facilities describes the "extraordinary" issues regarding college and university campuses in their recent annual report:

> From the holistic view this report affords of the challenges facing higher education institutions—notably large segments of aging building stock and flattening if not declining enrollment trends—it's extraordinary to see that many higher education decision-makers are choosing to add new buildings to their campuses. While our research indicates that institutions are taking steps to invest more strategically in facilities resources, the vast majority continue to underestimate the renewal needs of deteriorating spaces while pushing high-risk investments into new facilities.[14]

5 Campuses: Overvalued, Underused, and Very Costly   73

Clayton Christensen and Henry J. Eyring in *The Innovative University: Changing the DNA of Higher Education from the Inside Out* argue that educational technology and other factors place American institutions of higher education at great risk if they do not change. His concern is: "If they cannot find innovative, less costly ways of performing their uniquely valuable functions, they are doomed to decline, high global and national rankings notwithstanding." Colleges and universities must respond to the disruptive innovations if they are to meet the challenges of the future.[15]

Other concerned observers of US higher education are telling university leaders and their boards that higher education will have to become more flexible in order to respond to changing student needs. Busy, mobile lifestyles among older students especially will call for learning solutions that people can easily integrate into their daily lives. This will mean that the traditional role and function of the college campus will need to change to meet these dynamic and rapidly changing conditions.

Campuses will likely retain essential education spaces and facilities that students cannot provide for themselves such as laboratories, theaters, specialized equipment, research facilities, and libraries that have not yet digitized their collections. However, space for classrooms and lecture halls—the dominant use of campus space—will be less, perhaps, significantly less as ever larger percentages of students opt for on-line classes, experiential education, competency-based learning, study abroad, and other modes of active learning that do not require the traditional classroom.

The uncertainty of greatest concern surrounding the future of the college and university campus is not the changing conditions, needs, and expectations of the student marketplace. Rather, the uncertainty of greatest concern and the greatest risk lies with the higher education policy makers, governors, presidents, trustees, and leaders who must respond to these changes in a way that advances learning, meets the needs of the labor market, and promotes knowledge-based solutions to current problems. The future role and function of the college and university campus from the perspective of policy makers and university leaders appear to remain an open, unanswered question.

References

1. Tuan Nguyen, "The Effectiveness of Online Learning: Beyond No Significant Difference and Future Horizons," *Journal of Online Learning and Teaching* (Volume 11, Issue 2, June 2015), 309–319.
2. William Bowen, *The Cost Disease in Higher Education: Is Technology the Answer?* (The Tanner Lectures, Stanford University, October 2012).
3. Jonathan R. Cole, *Toward a More Perfect University* (New York: Public Affairs, 2016), 190.
4. John Marcus, The Paradox of New Buildings on Campus, *The Atlantic* (July 25, 2016).
5. James J. Duderstadt, Daniel E. Atkins, and Douglas Van Houwelling, *Higher Education in the Digital Age*, 9 (West Port, CT: Praeger Publishers, 2002), ix–x.
6. Amy Wang and Allison Schrager, *It's the End of the University as We Know It* (Quartz, September 27, 2017).
7. Ibid.
8. *The Economist*, June 27, 2014.
9. Julia Barr, *The Future of Education: The Virtual Campus* (SLICE.MIT.EDU, May 17, 2016).
10. Duderstadt et al., ibid.
11. *Chronicle of Higher Education*, December 3, 2017.
12. *Dayton Daily News*, February 24, 2016.
13. Julia Barr, ibid.
14. Sightlines, A Gordian Company.
15. Clay M. Christensen and Henry J. Eyring, *The Innovative University: Changing the DNA of Higher Education from the Inside Out* (San Francisco: Jossey-Bass, 2011).

6

Lectures, Textbooks, Academic Calendar, and Administration: An Agenda for Change

The old phrase, "Some things never change" may well be an exaggeration. However, notwithstanding the rapid and forceful change underway in nearly every part of modern society, some enclaves in our major institutions have proven highly resistant to change even when the need, advantages, and opportunities for change are well known and readily available.

This chapter identifies four of these "enclaves" in American higher education that have proven resistant to change—the lecture, textbooks, academic calendar, and administration—and makes the argument that this resistance and the mechanisms that protect them from change are weakening the educational experience and outcomes for students. This failure to change also comes at a high cost to students and their families in the form of rising tuition, mandatory fees, and unreasonable and unsustainable pricing. The questions for higher education leaders and policy makers are, When and how are these matters to be addressed? How long must twenty-first-century students live with and pay for costly, outmoded twentieth-century educational systems and practices? Where will the leadership come from to rid American public higher education of these costly anachronisms?

The Lecture

I was captivated recently by this interesting quote attributed to Samuel Johnson (1709–1784):

> "People have nowadays...got a strange opinion that everything should be taught by lectures. Now, I cannot see that lectures can do as much good as reading the books from which the lectures are taken. Lectures were once useful; but now, when all can read and books are so numerous, lectures are unnecessary."[1]

In the 1950s, the historian Henry Commager observed:

> Not only do we rely far too much on lectures, we rely on lectures to do far more than it is possible or desirable for them to do.[2]

Another interesting observation makes the point even clearer:

> A new study finds that undergraduate students in classes with traditional stand-and-deliver lectures are 1.5 times more likely to fail than students in classes that use more stimulating, so-called active learning methods.[3]

Scores of studies like this are coming out every year in all sorts of discipline journals. New studies as well as old going back decades, even centuries, agree and confirm, the lecture—our favorite and most common mode of instruction—may be the least effective mode for student learning. Whether it is mathematics, engineering, physics, nursing, or name the discipline, study after study tells us there are better, more effective ways to teach; indeed, some tell us the lecture is *no* way to advance learning. Ironically, we reject the findings and implications of our own empirical research when it applies to us. The lecture is a case in point.

Harvard physicist, Eric Mazur, takes us beyond the observations of critics and research when he says "...the impression I get is that it's almost unethical to be lecturing if you have data" showing how ineffective it is as a teaching and learning modality. Mazur has been campaigning against "stale lecturing techniques" for nearly three decades.[4]

The term "lecture" is derived from the Latin, to read aloud. Sometimes called the "sage on the stage"—lecturing is what those who study pedagogy refer to as "teacher-centered" instruction. Teacher-centered instruction is a mode of instruction that focuses on the instructor and his or her presentation. The model calls for students to listen carefully and take notes assuming the lecture material may appear in the form of questions on a test or final examination. The model also assumes that students will use their notes and study them to gain and retain information and knowledge of the subject.

Historically, the lecture was literally the only way to share information and knowledge when there were few if any books available to students. Professors stood before their students in the universities of Western Europe and read from the text since students had little or no access to this material. The practice continued, however, even as access to texts increased and books and other source materials became increasingly available to students. Today, the lecture still continues to serve as the primary mode of instruction—the sharing of information from a lectern in front of a hall or auditorium—despite the widespread availability of the same information in texts, journals, libraries, bookstores, and the internet.

Even with easy access to and availability of information, the lecture is defended as a proper, effective mode of instruction by many. Since my education experience was largely one of sitting in lecture halls and lecture classes, it was the model I emulated when I entered the teaching profession. Even as a graduate student many of my "seminars" were little more than informal lecture classes to a smaller number of students.

Most new college and university instructors use the same methods as their professors, i.e., they teach the way they were taught. My first years as a new assistant professor were devoted largely to lecture preparation and making sure my students got all the information required by the course. Much of the material I presented in my lectures could be easily found in the students' textbooks, on their reading lists or in the library. Even with all the information readily available, I believed it was my duty and my job to give lectures. I recall hearing stories about professors who gave such great lectures that their students would applaud at the end of the class. There were occasions I aspired to give such lectures. For me and my colleagues, college and lectures were one and the same.

I remember the old, not-so-funny definition of lecturing which went something like this: *Lecturing is the process of getting the notes from the professor's page to the student's page without passing through the brain of either.* A common and valid critique of lecturing is the *passive* nature of the method for students. It is this passive character of lecturing that renders it so ineffective. Student-centered instruction—a form of instruction that shifts the focus from *teaching* to *learning*—is more active and requires some form of engagement from the student rather than simply getting the information into their notes as accurately as possible.

Active, student-centered learning must somehow find a way to replace our tired, ineffective, passive, teacher-centered instruction. And, while the signs are encouraging, we have a long way to go before replacing the lecture as the dominant form of teaching. Experiential learning, service learning, cooperative learning, and other forms of active learning are giving students hands-on ways of learning and applying their new knowledge as well as gaining valuable experience and, happily for students, even gaining competence.

It is not the intent in this brief discussion of lectures to present even a summary of the decades of research and reflection that demonstrate the limitations, indeed the failures, of the lecture method. Study after study documents the "undisputed shortcomings" of the lecture. Yet, we persist in using the lecture method because that is the way the present-day professoriate was educated and, perhaps, more accurately, "the quickest and easiest way for a professor to discharge his nominal obligations as a teacher..." Page Smith, former provost at University of California Santa Cruz, summarized his views in this way: "I think it is fair to say that the lecture system is the most inefficient way of transmitting knowledge ever devised."[5]

Even more condemning than "inefficient" is the widespread view from students that lectures are boring. One study of student boredom suggests that almost 60% of students find at least half their lectures boring—with about 30% claiming to find most or all of their lectures boring.[6]

Institutions of higher education and academic professions have a responsibility to address this growing, inexcusable fault line that runs through their academic programs. Harvard's Eric Mazur is bringing the appropriate message to our universities when he argues that continuing to employ the lecture method in the face of all the evidence that it is ineffective is "unethical." In the context of the high cost of tuition, it is clearly wrong and arguably malfeasance for colleges and universities to require students to pay heavily and incur huge debts to receive a course of instruction using teaching methods that have been documented as "ineffective."

The irony, if not the tragedy, is the wealth of methods of teaching and learning available to the professoriate and their institutions. Decades of research, most of which has been conducted by university faculty, provide a rich inventory of teaching methods that bring documented effectiveness to the classroom. Technology is also giving us instructional tools today that could only be imagined a decade ago. Unfortunately, left to their own motivation, a large proportion of faculty have been slow adopting these new tools that, if adopted, could enhance student engagement and learning outcomes. Thoughtful critics of higher education continue to ask why these costly, ineffective practices persist? Clearly, the lecture method falls short of being student centered.

We need not necessarily think of the lecture method as a fatal crack in the higher education paradigm; however, the continued use of the traditional lecture is indicative of the resistance to or, at best, the slow pace of change in the one institution that should be *leading* change our society, i.e., universities. It is this slowness to adapt and even resistance to change that threatens our beloved universities and higher education more generally.

Textbooks

One of the many shocks students encounter during their first week on campus is at the checkout counter at their university bookstore. With four or five courses requiring a text or even multiple texts, the bookstore tab can run $1000 or more…each semester! Whoever thought a textbook could cost $250, $300 or more? There are reports of $400 chemistry texts! The College Board recommends that students budget $1200 a year for texts![7] That's an additional $4800 or more on top of the tuition, mandatory fees, room and board just for textbooks. This represents an 800% increase over the previous generation. Textbook costs are rapidly adding to the overall student debt. Sixty-five percent of students skip buying required texts at some point in their college career because of a lack of affordability. Some reports show that as many as 70% of college students now say they will not or cannot purchase one or more required textbooks due to cost concerns.

Even more concerning, prices in the college textbook market are increasing faster than the rate of inflation. One study shows the average cost of college textbooks has risen four times faster than the rate of inflation over the past 10 years.[8]

There are several unfortunate facts that contribute to the rising costs of textbooks: One of these is the revision cycle of many publishers. It is not uncommon for these cycles to be as short as 3 or 4 years. Many if not most faculty argue that these short revision cycles are unnecessary. New editions also limit the ability of students to sell their older edition books at the end of the semester. Ethan Senack, higher education advocate at Student Public Interest Research Groups, describes the prices of textbooks as "a serious problem."

> We've known for a long time that high textbook prices create a lose-lose choice for students. They can either spend hundreds of dollars to buy the textbook, take time away from studying to work extra hours to pay for their books, or they can go without the book and accept the consequences.[9]

Along with the traditional textbooks, many college classes now require students to purchase access codes—which typically cost $100 on average—to online platforms created by major publishers. Homework and quizzes are also placed on the platforms behind paywalls that expire at the end of each semester, meaning students can't resell them once they're done with the course. Roughly 60% of students used an access code during the 2016–2017 academic year, according to the National Association of College Stores (NACS).

Students feel trapped by the access code system with some claiming "There doesn't seem to be any way around it," and now "you have to pay to do homework." A. J. Goldman, general manager for textbooks at Chegg, a Web site that seeks to make college more affordable and accessible, says "the No. 1 concern that I hear [from students] over and over is pricing." He said it's common for students to have to buy a $500 textbook and $100 access code for a single course and lamented how much of a burden that is for many students.

> $5 makes a difference, it's the cost of a meal. Nontraditional students account for a majority of today's college-going population, some of them single mothers who are working 40 hours a week while taking night classes and taking care of their kids. The difference between spending $80 and $100 on a book is serious money for them…It's an hour of work.[10]

Its estimated that the nation's 5.2 million undergraduate students who receive financial aid spend about $3 billion annually on textbooks and codes. According to *NBC*'s review of Bureau of Labor Statistics (BLS) data, textbook prices have risen over three times the rate of inflation from January 1977 to June 2015, a 1041% increase.[11] Nicole Allen, spokesperson for the Scholarly Publishing and Academic Resources Coalition says "They've been able to keep raising prices because students are 'captive consumers.' They have to buy whatever books they're assigned."[12]

A University of Michigan (2009) study of the problem reveals other factors contributing to the increasing cost of textbooks. More publishers are now adding or "bundling" other materials with the text that add to the cost including workbooks, software, and study guides.[13]

Greater use of new or different approaches including open educational materials, open resources, and other online sources could substantially reduce the cost of texts. Digitally licensed e-books can also reduce costs. Institutions that are truly "student centered" will see this as a major concern and begin now, working with other institutions of higher education and higher education associations, to address the problem with cost-effective, innovative strategies, and long-term solutions. University leaders, including boards of trustees, need to be aware of the cost of college textbooks and engaged in efforts to reduce the severe financial impact on students. Responsible boards will set aside time to review the textbook issue and lending their support to more cost-effective strategies for students.

Ethan Senack, a federal higher education advocate for US Public Interest Research Group, responding to questions about rising textbook prices had this to say:

> Textbooks are so expensive because professors assign specific editions and just five publishers have a lock on the market. That means they're able to drive up prices without fear of market competitors. The content of some courses changes, but not nearly enough to justify brand new print editions—sometimes every two years—that carry such high prices.[14]

This is part of the broken higher education paradigm for which students are paying unreasonable and unfair prices. The days of the $200 and $300 textbooks are just one more assault on students and university leaders owe it to their students to find a more cost conscious approach to the textbook scam.

The Academic Calendar

The academic calendar at most colleges and universities, while not quite a "sacred cow," has a robust status among campus traditions that makes it difficult, if not impossible, to change. Historians offer somewhat different explanations for the academic calendar with most suggesting its origins lie with the needs of families during an agrarian era. Whatever the origins, most calendars begin the academic year in the fall—late August to mid-September—and end in May or early June.

There are basically three types of academic calendars currently serving institutions of higher education in the USA: semester, quarter, and trimester. The semester system divides the academic year into two terms of equal length and often an optional summer session half as long as a full semester. Spring and fall semesters provide 32–36 weeks of instruction.

The quarter system divides the academic year into four terms, one per season, with three quarters providing 32–36 weeks of instruction. The trimester system divides the academic year into three terms of 14–16 weeks each, with 28–32 weeks of instruction. The trimester, a variant of the semester, gained limited acceptance in the 1960s, with the aim of standardizing periods of study and encouraging more year-round attendance with shorter time to complete a degree.

According to data provided by the NACS, 71.2% of the 4373 institutions it surveyed in 2011 were on a semester calendar. Only 14.7% of colleges used quarters. Other institutions use trimesters and other less common schedules.[15] The American Association of College Registrars and Admissions Officers also tracked the use of the semester calendar between 1990 and 2001. Their study found the percentage of institutions using a semester calendar increased from 62 to 70% in those 11 years. The move toward the semester system continued in the following years but at a slower rate making the semester the dominant structural unit for academic calendars.[16]

The decision to transition from one academic calendar system to another is fairly complex, sometimes difficult and requires many adjustments, i.e., personnel changes, payroll, class schedules, transcripts, and more. Colleges and universities making the change from the quarter system to the semester calendar cite their hopes for encouraging transfers from institutions using the dominant calendar—particularly community colleges—as well as increasing internships and study abroad opportunities.

Despite efforts of colleges and universities to find the right system "fit" for their students, the fact remains that the academic calendar is a lingering remnant of academic credit, a "seat-time" measure of learning and progress toward a degree. Clearly, some form of calendar or structure is needed to organize the offerings of colleges and universities; however, opportunities for greater creativity and innovation exist and are needed to design an academic calendar that will encourage a faster time to the degree, meet the needs of non-traditional students, promote a more "competency-based" system and take full advantage of the technologies available that can reduce the investment of time and money. Perhaps, it is time to even reconsider the concept of "class" and class schedule as the basis for the academic calendar. The inertia of these century-long traditions and structures creates barriers and obstacles to new, more creative, flexible, individualistic, and customized approaches to higher education.

One of the most important calendar-related issues in higher education is the "time to degree." Over the past several decades we have, for example, substituted the phrase, "four-year degree" for baccalaureate degree. We have virtually abandoned the word, baccalaureate, outside formal writing or discussions. We also know that, for an increasing number of students, it takes six years to earn a four-year degree adding significantly to the cost of their college years. And, colleges and universities measure their (four-year) graduation rates using a six year completion period.

In 2010, Stephen Trachtenberg and Gerald Kauvar, in a *New York Times* op ed piece (May 24, 2010), challenged the assumptions behind the four-year degree. They argued "The college experience may be idyllic, but it's also wasteful and expensive, both for students and institutions. There is simply no reason undergraduate degrees can't be finished in three years, and many reasons they should be."[17] Their challenge has helped spark a renewed conversation about our assumptions regarding the time required for a degree which has, in turn, led to new thinking and approaches to the academic calendar.

Like so many anachronistic traditions in American higher education, it is now time—still early in the twenty-first century—to move forward with a new, more creative and flexible approach to the academic calendar that structures learning opportunities and recognizes individual competency and knowledge as the basis for certification and the awarding of degrees. It may even be time to rethink the notion of a college "degree" in light of the needs, demands, and desires of students of all types as well as the needs of the workplace and society.

Administration

Remember Walt Kelly's famous line in Pogo "*We have met the enemy and he is us?*" This cartoon appeared in a 1970 antipollution poster for Earth Day and quickly captured the collective imagination of Americans. It is still a popular line and is widely used in everyday conversations as well as public discourse. It had a ring of truth when Kelly first used the line and that ring of truth still fits so many of today's issues and challenges. We can be and often are our own worst enemies. That may well be the case in higher education administration.

Many of the issues, including problems and challenges facing higher education, lie in the nature, size, and execution of college and university administration. Higher education administration has become the source of considerable controversy, concern, and criticism over the past few decades for several reasons. First is the rapid growth in the number of administrative positions. The number of non-academic administrative and professional employees at US colleges and universities has more than doubled in the last 25 years, vastly outpacing the growth in the number of students or faculty. From 1987 until 2011–2012 universities and colleges collectively added 517,636 administrators and professional employees, or an average of 87 every working day, according to the New England Center for Investigative Reporting and American Institutes for Research. In presenting these findings, Andrew Gillen, senior researcher at the Institutes said, "There's just a mind-boggling amount of money per student that's being spent on administration. It raises a question of priorities."[18] The sheer growth of college and university administration begs a number of important questions that are not being addressed or even asked.

Second, and closely related to the first concern, is the cost of administration. Accounting differences and complexities make it difficult to get a good fix on the actual cost of administration. There is a general consensus that the cost of administration has risen substantially over the past decade; the differences are in the actual amount of the increases. Some argue that increases in the cost of administration may be as low as 5%. Others describe the increases as "steep."

A *Huffington Post* analysis of higher education administrators cites the work of Richard Vedder, an economist and director of the Center for College Affordability and Productivity. In response to the insistence that university presidents are "doing everything they can to improve efficiency and hold down costs" Vedder responds, "It's a lie. It's a lie. It's a lie…I wouldn't buy a used car from a university president…They'll say,

'We're making moves to cut costs,' and mention something about energy-efficient lightbulbs, and ignore the new assistant to the assistant to the associate vice provost they just hired."[19]

The California State University system, while not necessarily representative of other higher education systems, is illustrative of the growth of university administration. A 2017 personnel audit, requested by the California Joint Legislative Audit Committee, found CSU's workforce includes different categories of employees, including 30 executives, nearly 4000 management personnel, about 21,400 faculty, and nearly 26,900 non-faculty support staff. The audit report concludes that "growth in the number and compensation of management personnel significantly outpaced those of other employee types, including non-faculty support staff." Of even greater significance and interest, the six campuses visited as part of the audit frequently could not justify the growth in the number of new management personnel. This Cal State audit identified other irregularities including unsupported increases in pay for campus managers.[20]

Other practices raise questions if not concerns with respect to the lack of experience or training in management of many academic faculty appointed to administrative positions. Most academics filling positions in university administration are not trained in administration or management nor prepared for these roles. For the great majority of faculty—all of whom are well educated in various disciplines—administration is seldom one of their strengths or competencies. Many faculty take great pride in the fact that they are not administrators or managers and joke about those who do get drawn, often by 12 month contracts and larger salaries, to "the dark side" of administration.

One of the consequences of this lack of training in administration and management is that many of the tasks involved in running an administrative unit in a large complex organization such as universities are carried out very inefficiently. The cost of this inefficiency has never been fully calculated. This lack of training for management and administration is frequently accompanied by a lack of confidence in management decisions. It also means that it may take two or three times as many people to perform an administrative or management task that could be done by one properly trained professional.

There is no requirement or even expectation that professors selected for administrative and management positions—often by other professors—seek any training for their new role. Nearly all of the preparation for these administrative jobs is "on the job training." The signs of this lack of training and preparation are ubiquitous throughout university administration and reflected in the high cost of administration. On the job training is slow and frequently less than adequate for the efficient and effective operation of the institution. Conferences and consultants help address these inadequacies but with an added cost in time and money.

This is a resolvable problem if there is the institutional insight, will and leadership to address it. The resolution of this deeply institutionalized weakness may require changes in the academic culture; however, a genuine student-centered system of higher education should welcome such changes.

Conclusion: Agenda for Change

If higher education ever honestly develops an "agenda for change," these topics—the lecture, textbooks, academic calendar, and administration—would be high priorities. All four are long-standing mainstays in American colleges and universities but are now becoming obstacles to cost-effective and affordable higher education. Each in its own way has become a costly distraction to students' quest for a college education.

The institutional inertia and lack of change on these issues in the face of decades of research documenting the problems and need for change continues to represent a great opportunity for developing genuine student-centered colleges and universities. Governors are in a position to encourage and even insist that their public institutions become more student centered. Governing boards and trustees are also well-positioned and responsible for raising questions about how their colleges and universities can become more student centered. University presidents are in positions of leadership that should be demanding action on the major issues and problems underlying ever more costly tuition and fees for students. Higher education associations are also well-positioned to nurture national conversations with colleges and universities on these topics and to help move the nation's institutions toward the needed reforms for the twenty-first century.

Changing these deeply entrenched practices and traditions on the nation's college and university campuses will not be easy and will require exceptionally strong leadership. Because of the complexity of these issues, it is important that those charged with the responsibility of leading and stewarding the nation's public institutions of higher education begin soon to lay out an agenda for change. Each year, America's institutions of higher education become more costly and self-serving rather than serving the needs and interests of students for whom the colleges and universities were created. Most colleges and universities claim to be student centered. It is time we make good on that claim.

References

1. Tony Bates. "Why Lectures Are Dead (Or Soon Will Be)," *Online Learning and Distance Education Resources* (July 27, 2014).
2. Henry S. Commager, "The Problem Isn't Bricks—Its Brains," *New York Times Magazine* (January 19, 1956, cited in Paul Christine and Matthew Rysavy, *Lectures and the Hidden Curriculum*, deepblue.lib.umich.edu).
3. Alleszu Bajak, "Lectures Aren't Just Boring: They're Ineffective Too, Study Finds," *Science* (May 12, 2014).
4. Ibid.
5. Page Smith, *Killing the Spirit* (New York: Viking Penguin, 1990), 215.
6. *The Guardian* (May 11, 2009).
7. College Board, *Trends in College Pricing* (2013).
8. Ben Popkin, "College Textbook Prices Have Risen 1041 Percent Since 1977," *NBC News* (August 6, 2015).
9. Herb Weisbaum, "Students Are Still Saddled with Soaring Textbook Costs, Report Says," *NBC News* (February 10, 2016).
10. Laura McKenna, "Why Students Are Still Spending So Much for College Textbooks," *The Atlantic* (January 26, 2018).
11. Ben Popkin, ibid.
12. Abby Jackson, "One of the Biggest Ways College Students Are Ripped Off Is Getting Out of Control," *Business Insider* (August 3, 2015).

13. Natsuko Hayashi Nicholls, *Rising Textbook Expenses and a Search for Solutions: Survey and Interview Results from Michigan Faculty* (Scholarly Publishing Office, University of Michigan Library, 2009).
14. "Here's Exactly Why College Textbooks Are So Expensive," *ATTN* (March 12, 2015).
15. Mitch Smith, "Strength in Numbers," *Inside Higher Ed* (February 12, 2012).
16. Ibid.
17. Stephen Trachtenberg and Gerald Kauvar, "A Degree in Three," *New York Times* (May 24, 2010).
18. Quoted in Jon Marcus, "News Analysis Shows Problematic Boom in Higher Education Administrators," *HuffPost* (February 6, 2014).
19. Ibid.
20. *California State University: Stronger Oversight Is Needed for Hiring and Compensating Management Personnel and for Monitoring Campus Budgets* (California State Auditor, Report 2016-122).

7

Duplication of Programs: Where Do We Draw the Line?

Throughout my career in higher education administration, I have observed close up costly duplication of services, programs, and even entire universities. In the early 1990s, for example, I served as a dean at the University of North Texas (UNT) located in Denton at the northern edge of the Dallas-Fort Worth Metroplex. A six-minute, 1.6-mile drive from the UNT campus is Texas Woman's University (TWU). Like UNT, TWU is a public, state-supported university. In 1972, TWU began admitting male students and is now a coeducational university where in 2014 a male student was elected student body president.

A decade later I was invited to join the University of Toledo (Ohio) as president. Upon arriving, I found we had an important public, state-supported university neighbor, Bowling Green State University, just 25 minutes from our campus. In both instances, there were two public, state-supported universities located just minutes apart. The proximity and duplication of programs, services, and sports in the neighboring tax-supported universities had not escaped public attention or scrutiny. Although each campus had its alumni and constituents as well as enthusiastic fans of their sports teams, many questioned the wisdom and need for locating two comprehensive, state-supported

© The Author(s) 2019
D. M. Johnson, *The Uncertain Future of American Public Higher Education*,
https://doi.org/10.1007/978-3-030-01794-1_7

public universities within minutes of each other. Public officials and policy analysts, through their inaction, appear to be satisfied that the proximity and duplication of nearly all the programs and services is good education and public policy that justifies the duplicated expenditures. The question is, are they correct? Is this sound education and public policy? Many will argue—at least from a fiscal perspective—that such policies are not only inefficient but wasteful of taxpayer funds.

During our times at UNT and University of Toledo, the propinquity of these tax-supported institutions was a frequent topic of discussion. Occasionally, serious questions were raised about the rationale of having two tax-supported public universities that duplicate each other in nearly every respect located within minutes of one another. Duplicated administrations from president and provost down to assistant deans and department chairs, duplicated libraries, largely duplicated curricula, duplicated faculty expertise, duplicated classrooms and labs, duplicated athletic facilities, duplicated dining halls and student residences were a fact of university life. Unnecessary duplications in other areas including human resources and personnel, attorneys, information technology, health clinics, transportation, and more added to the costs that ultimately were borne by students, their families and the taxpaying citizens of the states.

These two instances in my own experience are a mere fraction of the nation's public, state-supported colleges and universities that are located within minutes of a second, large public-supported university with all the duplications inherent in such co-located institutions. One could reasonably ask, "Is this duplication really necessary or is it unnecessary duplication?" If you ask members of the respective campuses, their administrations, trustees, and alumni, the answer is almost always, this duplication is needed, justified and valuable and must remain. If you ask objective policy makers and taxpayers who foot the bills for the duplicated facilities, faculties, and services, it is very likely that they see this as not only unnecessary but irresponsible and irrational, costly public policy and an unaffordable luxury that needs to be addressed.

How Many Education, Business, and Engineering Programs Do We Need?

Duplication of university programs is a very touchy political subject. Significant, costly, unnecessary duplication of academic programs, colleges, and even whole universities are a giant fact of life in American higher education. The extent of duplication has never been fully studied or audited although some states are now raising questions about the extent of duplication and the portion of duplication that most reasonable people might agree is "unnecessary." For example, how many law schools, colleges of engineering, pharmacy schools, and criminal justice programs are needed in a state? How many Ph.D. programs in English, art history, and linguistics are needed in states to produce the next generation of university faculty? And, how do higher education policy makers and university trustees view this duplication? More importantly, why do they continue to give an unquestioned "green light" to the continuation of these programs, seemingly without regard to the cost to their university or availability of jobs for graduates from these programs?

Public colleges and universities and the states that support them that are serious about cutting the cost of higher education, know that the most fruitful places to look for savings is the duplication of courses, minors, majors, graduate programs, departments, schools, colleges, and even entire universities. Many states have taken steps—some dating back three decades or longer—to avoid unnecessary duplication of *new* programs. Systems offices, state higher education officers, higher education coordinating boards, and other central authorities have instituted policies to guard against unnecessary academic program duplication. Some states have put into place rigorous multilevel review processes and procedures to help ensure that duplication of proposed courses and programs are identified and that unnecessary duplication be addressed either through non-approvals or collaboration with existing programs. Other states leave it to the proposing department or school to judge the degree of duplication as well as decide if the duplication is unnecessary.

The major weakness of the current approach to identifying, limiting, or stopping unnecessary duplication is that it never became retroactive; only *new* courses or programs are subject to the duplication review process. Scores, if not hundreds, of programs in nearly all states have, in effect, been grandfathered into long-established curricula without review or scrutiny of the degree to which they duplicate programs at nearby institutions. Few, if any, universities have audited existing programs to determine the full scope of duplication. An objective study of student demand and cost-benefit for these programs—preferably by a qualified, neutral outside party—would form the basis for a sound determination of the extent and cost of unnecessary duplication.

However, even with valid data in hand, reducing or eliminating unnecessary duplication of university programs can be very difficult or nearly impossible with all the protections against outside intrusion built into our system. Long-standing curricula have provided the rationale for hiring, reappointments, and tenuring of faculty. Elaborate policies and procedures for eliminating a course, reducing or eliminating programs are permanent fixtures in governance handbooks and academic cultures that virtually guarantee uninterrupted continuation of curricula and programs. Students enrolled in these programs have been given assurance by their university bulletins and catalogs that their programs will continue and be in place for their graduation. The challenges and complexities surrounding the reduction or elimination of programs are daunting to the extent that few universities are inclined to pursue this course of action short of financial exigency.

Unnecessary duplication goes on not only between universities but *within* universities. On many university campuses, for example, academic departments often demand their own statistics courses. I recall heated discussions in the 1970s and 1980s in which our department fought to keep our own statistics courses, taught by our own statistician. The end result is the costly multiplication of statistics courses with the same general content being taught in Psychology, Sociology, Economics, Business, Engineering, and other departments and schools.

Who Pays for This Duplication?

Within university duplication pales in comparison with the costly duplication of programs, schools, and colleges that exists *between* and among our universities. The concern here is primarily with our public, tax-supported universities that persist in justifying costly duplicative programs even at institutions located in close proximity to each other. Having multiple colleges of education, business, and other professional schools serving the same region and constituencies, competing for the same students, faculty, research grants, and donors makes little sense from an, fiscal, or philanthropic policy perspective. Yet, the practice continues without challenge. More problematic, these duplications increase the cost of higher education that is passed on to students in their tuition and to taxpayers.

The cost of multiplication and unnecessary duplication of academic programs among our tax-supported public universities has not been calculated, but it is now time to calculate the cost. When it is studied and we know the cost, we will find that duplicate programs in many states run into the hundreds of millions of dollars…dollars that could be applied to improving the quality of other, non-duplicated programs.

The current paradigm for public higher education recognizes and rewards *quantity* of programs rather than quality. From a policy perspective, it is easy to envision the benefits of closing weak academic programs and colleges and investing the savings in making strong programs stronger, more competitive. To their credit, some universities—either voluntarily or out of necessity—are moving forward with the heavy lifting of setting priorities for their institutions. It is increasingly understood, that universities cannot be "all things to all people."

Setting Priorities

It is a poorly kept secret that our colleges and universities offer many duplicative programs. It is also recognized that many of these programs are not based on "need" as much as historical legacies, institutional egos and desire to offer any course or program any person may want in order to capture as many credit hours possible. It is also becoming increasingly obvious that our universities and the states that support them can ill-afford such costly, duplicative programs. Continuing support of the scores of costly duplicated programs and services adds to the tuition paid by students and the subsidy provided by the taxpayers of our states. This is a luxury for our colleges and universities—indeed all of higher education—but not a sustainable model that students or taxpayers can afford.

Nearly two decades ago, Robert C. Dickeson, a former college president and foundation official, published a small but powerful treatise on this subject, *Prioritizing Academic Programs and Services: Reallocating Resources to Achieve Strategic Balance*.[1] It is a book every university policy maker and senior administrator needs to incorporate in their strategic planning process and program decision-making. Dickeson argues forcefully and, in my view, correctly that it is long past time for our colleges and universities to bite the bullet and begin setting priorities for our programs and services. "It is possible" he writes, "to identify and eliminate unnecessary duplication of programs and resource-draining deadwood."[2] For our public universities, it is not only sound academic policy but necessary public policy.

The necessity for resetting academic priorities is the result of the historic tendency of universities "to add and not to delete, to plant and not prune." The curricula of many—perhaps most—academic departments and colleges is a legacy of accumulated decisions by different departmental actors over multiple decades and longer. These decisions reflect the needs, interests, challenges, or opportunities at the time the program or courses were adopted; to complicate matters, the theoretical perspectives undergirding the evolving curricula and programs also reflected the dominant theories and studies of the period. But times and the needs of society change; for better or worse, university programs are slow to change. Those that joke about such matters have said, "If you believe in reincarnation, come back as an academic program and enjoy eternal life."[3]

Calculating the Cost

With the evolution of the university and the creation of its programs and services over the past century has come the continuing growth of faculty and staff, construction of facilities to house these programs, and a proliferation of administrative positions to oversee and supervise the growing body of programs and services. This growth in personnel, programs, and facilities—as well as all the indirect costs associated with this growth—has driven costs and expenditures ever higher at an ever accelerating rate. New and expanding sources of revenue were identified and, for the most part, kept pace with rising expenditures through the latter half of the twentieth century, albeit with increasing difficulty. Tuition increases, capital campaigns, expansion of grant-seeking efforts, new student fees, tapping endowments, corporate sponsorships, and enhanced searches for non-traditional sources of revenue fed the efforts to help balance the growing expenditure column in university budgets.

With the visible and very real limits to increasing revenue, and for public universities the realization that state subsidies will continue to shrink, the time for cutting expenditures has arrived. Throughout my years in administration as a department chair, college dean, and provost, we usually approached the need to cut expenditures by across-the-board budget reductions, not filling vacated positions, deferring equipment purchases or needed maintenance, and eliminating all but absolutely essential travel. No judgments of the relative importance of courses, programs, or services were needed, wanted nor made. These strategies were simply designed to balance the budget as painlessly as possible with as little disruption as possible and get the department, college, and even the university through the fiscal year. We would deal with next year's budget shortfall next year…using the same strategies.

These stopgap measures are no longer sufficient, adequate, or appropriate to address the ballooning budgets of our colleges and universities. Two decades ago, the Commission on National Investment in Higher Education (1997) described the fiscal situation as a "time bomb" ready to inflict permanent damage to the important functions of our nation's universities. The call for "major structural changes" in higher education, a call that had been made countless times by scores of caring higher education policy analysts, has gone unheeded. That "time bomb" has now exploded and the fallout is profoundly evident in the ballooning trillion-dollar student loans and lifetime indebtedness of our college and university graduates. It is evident in the attitudes of state legislators frustrated by the demands of their public university presidents and governing boards for more and better of everything, without limits.

This frustration is also evident in many sectors of the business community that are seeking graduates with basic skills to fill important roles but with limited success.

Going beyond his call for presidents and their governing boards to prioritize programs and services, Dickeson brings an even more compelling message: "...there is a fundamental need to reform. The status quo is unacceptable."[4] What is it going to take to reform a broken system and create one that genuinely works putting students first?

Community College Four-Year Degrees: More Duplication

A classic example of creating costly duplicative programs is the initiative of community colleges in several states to offer four-year degrees. Currently, there are approximately 90 community colleges offering 700 four-year degree programs in 19 states with more degrees waiting to be approved. The rationale for authorizing two-year community colleges to expand includes providing access to baccalaureate degrees in areas not previously available, providing low-cost degrees to compete with the more expensive four-year university programs, and providing graduates in targeted, labor-shortage areas.[5]

The intended objective of authorizing the two-year colleges to offer four-year degrees is understandable and, on the surface, appears to solve one of the major issues in higher education, i.e., lower cost. Community colleges have been advocating for the authority to offer four-year degrees for several years as a way of maintaining and increasing their enrollments. The unintended consequence of this initiative, however, is increased competition for students and increased demands for state funding for higher education at a time when students and funding are already in short supply.

There is no question that the costs for the two-year community colleges will increase with the adoption of four-year degrees. Four-year degrees are more costly to offer than two-year degrees. The Michigan Association of State Universities, where four-year degrees for

7 Duplication of Programs: Where Do We Draw the Line?

community colleges are being considered, forecasts the likely outcome if degree authority is granted:

> In duplicating already-existing four-year programs available at the state's public universities, community colleges will incur costs for salary and benefits of additional faculty and support staff, as well as operating costs for administration, materials and supplies, travel, information technology, meeting accreditation requirements and providing other support services. Capital expenses related to equipment and facilities may also be incurred.[6]

In addition to these requests for larger state appropriations, it should also be anticipated that duplicating baccalaureate degrees in community colleges will add to local taxation through higher millages. With a larger percentage of students selecting the community college route to a baccalaureate degree, costs for students seeking their four-year degrees at universities will also likely increase due to lower enrollments and the lost benefits from economies of scale.

The community college movement to offer four-year degrees is, in large measure, a reflection of the failure of universities to manage costs and offer affordable degree programs. If community colleges continue to pursue this course and are given authority to offer four-year degrees, the overall system of higher education is not only weakened, it will increase costs substantially and indefinitely. This duplicative move will, over the long term, drive tuition prices even higher for both the community colleges and the universities.

Public colleges and universities have known about the ambitions of community colleges to move into the baccalaureate student market for years if not decades. University resistance to changing market conditions and compelling economic realities will, with the four-year community college degree programs tapping into the student market, exacerbate the challenges to an already weakened higher education infrastructure and paradigm.

Unfortunately, there are those in public and other four-year universities that continue to argue that succumbing to market pressures, management strategies and "economic rationality" will be "a detriment to the longer-term educational legacies and democratic interests that have long characterized American public education."[7] What is not recognized in this perspective is that by *not* adopting economic rationality, recognizing market pressures, and improving management, our public universities will not survive, certainly not in their present form.

More Collaboration and Less Duplication

Universities are not natural collaborators. For many in higher education, collaboration is an *unnatural* act. Most faculty are more interested in "doing their own thing" rather than investing in ventures and projects that take time away from their personal and professional activities and interests, even if these investments lead to more productive institutional outcomes. Departments and colleges as well as universities have been reluctant collaborators for much of their history. Being risk averse, turf conscious and playing it safe and selfishly have prevented institutions of higher education from capturing the significant rewards of collaboration and adding value to the investment in public higher education.

Mounting pressures from state legislatures as well as increasing opportunities with business and industry have led a growing number of universities into the collaborative arena. Conference proceedings and a growing body of literature in academic and scholarly publications documenting the benefits and payoffs of collaborative programs and projects are enticing more faculty, departments, colleges, and whole institutions into collaborative ventures. "Collaborative leadership" is an increasingly common phrase in position descriptions for deans, provosts, and presidents.

For some institutions, collaboration has become an economic imperative. In addition to the intrinsic value of collaboration, it is also an effective way of cutting costs among collaborating public universities. Typical of a growing number of university systems, the Iowa Board of Regents, recently released a summary of a consultant's report that found collaboration opportunities among their three universities—University of Iowa, Iowa State University, and University of Northern Iowa—and pointed to "overlapping and duplication of roles, services and programs." The report reveals ways the three institutions could save significant costs through changing purchasing practices, using buildings more effectively and savings in utility costs.

The Iowa example is reflective of many, perhaps most, states. Significant "overlapping and duplication of roles, services and programs" is ubiquitous but more importantly, unnecessarily costly. These overlapping and duplicated programs must be paid for. Frequently, the price of these unneeded programs diverts funds from needed programs that, with a small infusion of funds, could become significantly stronger or, perhaps, truly outstanding. There is also a growing feeling and perception among taxpayers that they are paying for many very similar programs, some of which are unnecessarily duplicative.

Ohio is another example: The Ohio Department of Higher Education (DHE) established a course and program sharing network that allows Ohio's public colleges and universities and adult career centers to share curricula for existing courses and academic programs. The purpose of the program sharing network was to "avoid program duplication." Their report, "How-To Guide: Sharing Courses and Programs at Ohio's Colleges and Universities," shows how the network "allows two or more campuses to work in collaboration to deliver programming that specifically addresses business and/or industry needs and to meet those needs efficiently."[8]

The Texas A&M Academic Common Market (ACM) is another example of encouraging inter-institutional collaboration as a way of eliminating unnecessary duplication. The ACM accomplishes this objective through an exchange of students across state borders at in-state rates. Through the Common Market, universities support existing degree programs that have the capacity to serve additional students, provide greater access to existing degree programs, and open windows of opportunity for institutions to find collaborative ways to better serve students of the region at less cost.

Collaboration offers an effective first step in addressing the problems of unnecessary duplication. States owe it to their citizens, taxpayers, and students to seek opportunities for efficiency-generating, inter-institutional collaboration. Governors can play an important strategic leadership role in fostering collaboration among their state-subsidized colleges and universities. In most states, governors appoint college and university trustees. If these appointments came with a word or letter from the governor encouraging their new trustees to seek opportunities for meaningful collaboration, collaboration would likely become more common and, perhaps, the norm. If trustees were encouraged by the governors to identify and eliminate unnecessary duplication, it would become an active discussion at governing board meetings that would, in all likelihood, lead to cost-saving measures.

In some cases, leaders, governing boards, and policy makers may find opportunities to go beyond collaboration in their search for less duplicative, more cost-effective models for higher education. A model of increasing interest is a merger of two or more institutions; such actions offer opportunities to reduce or eliminate whole departments and achieve significant cost savings that benefit students and taxpayers. Stand-alone medical schools, law schools, schools of dentistry, and other professional institutions may well find greater strength and sustainability by merging with a nearby university. Entire universities may soon find that merging is the only path to sustainability.

An interesting and effective model of a recent merger is the University of Toledo and the Medical University of Ohio. In 2006, the Medical University of Ohio merged with the University of Toledo creating the third largest public university in Ohio. Following a period of intense discussions and planning, the boards of trustees of the two institutions sought legislative approval for the merger. The Ohio legislature enthusiastically approved the merger without a single dissenting vote.

Collaboration alone will not solve the deeply engrained and fully institutionalized duplication of programs and services. However, collaboration creates opportunities for dialogue, enhanced cooperation, problem solving and, potentially, cost savings that can be passed on to those who fund our colleges and universities and pay for its programs.

Conclusions

Academic programs, services and, indeed, whole institutions are widely and unnecessarily duplicated across the nation's higher education landscape. The total cost of this redundancy is not known but the extent of unnecessary duplication of programs and services is an important cost consideration for every state: unnecessary duplication is a significant, but invisible, expenditure line in every state and university budget. In some states, the cost of unnecessary academic redundancy can annually exceed tens or even hundreds of millions of dollars in larger states.

Although there are policies and procedures in most states to protect against future unnecessary duplication of programs, the horses were out of the barn before such protections were put in place. The tragedy of this needless duplication is the high cost it imposes on students, their families, and taxpayers. The current system and paradigm that supports "bundled" public higher education in the USA requires students to pay for more than they receive or even want.

It is unrealistic to expect our public colleges and universities alone to address this problem in a serious or effective way. Unraveling unnecessary program and service duplication is a complex undertaking; any fully committed attempt to rid a university of unnecessary duplication—much less an entire state system—could well be a decade-long or longer process. But, with the political will and effective leadership, it could be accomplished.

Gail M. Morrison writes about the complexity of changing academic programs and the challenges of ridding the system of its academic redundancy. Those who have studied or are familiar with the problem will likely agree with her analysis. Morrison states that:

> ...unnecessary program duplication is not so simple a concept as it might seem. Rather, academic program offerings are fluid and responsive to complex interactions among student demand, employer needs, faculty and institutional strengths, cost-benefit relationships, the emergence of new disciplines, the decline of older disciplines, and community development and enrichment, among other factors. Issues of access and quality must be balanced against degree and enrollment productivity. Greater flexibility is accorded to establishing undergraduate programs than to doctoral programs while master's programs enjoy greater or lesser flexibility depending on whether they serve place-bound professionals or not.[9]

Building a collaborative future, while very important, will not dissolve the century-long legacy of unnecessary duplications built into the system. New creative structures, incentives, and perhaps, a new vision is needed for meeting the higher education needs of society that lowers costs, improves quality, and advances competency among students. We know the problems well; the higher education literature of the past half decade has documented the challenges facing our systems. It is now our task to reform higher education in a manner that advances collaboration and eliminates unnecessary duplication.

I would be remiss if I failed to acknowledge the efforts of many major institutions and states to address the challenges of unnecessary duplication. Indeed, there are many such well-intentioned efforts underway. Even if these efforts are successful, their successes will be limited to minor, marginal gains in protecting against *future* duplication. The problem of program duplication and unnecessary redundancy is structural, systemic, and well institutionalized; the paradigmatic infrastructure upon which American higher education rests requires major reform and restructuring. The incentives, motivations, and incremental add-ons in their present forms can only lead to more of the same or worse.

References

1. Robert C. Dickeson, *Prioritizing Academic Programs: Reallocating Resources to Achieve Strategic Balance* (Jossey-Bass: 1999).
2. Ibid., p. 125.
3. Ibid., p. 43.
4. Ibid., p. 9.
5. Ellen Marrison, "Community Colleges Continuing Trend to Offer Four-year Degrees," *SSTI Digest* (December 20, 2017).
6. *Collaboration Versus Duplication as the Model for Michigan Public Higher Education,* Michigan Association of State Universities (no date).
7. Patricia Gumport, "Academic Restructuring: Organizational Chang and Institutional Imperatives," *Higher Education* (volume 39, 2000), 67–91.
8. "How-To Guide: Sharing Courses/Programs at Ohio's Colleges and Universities," *Ohio Department of Higher Education* (September, 2017).
9. Gail M. Morrison, "Perspectives on Program Duplication," *South Carolina Commission on Higher Education* (May 28, 2010), 5.

8

Intercollegiate Athletics: Challenge to the Academic Mission

American universities have been captured and are being held hostage by intercollegiate athletics, major athletic conferences, and the National Collegiate Athletic Association (NCAA). The failure of university governing boards and presidents to reign in costs and bring greater balance between athletics and academics has led observers and critics to view university leaders as co-conspirators and active partners in this capture. The loss of control of intercollegiate athletics by universities to the unbridled vagaries of the sports marketplace driven by infusions of big money from television, sponsors, and a host of other sources, known and unknown, has weakened our universities' capacity to fully realize their *academic* missions and added massive amounts of debt to their students. To many concerned observers, athletic department priorities and intercollegiate sports frequently trump the academic missions of their universities.

Many university leaders and sports enthusiasts alike view the current trends and economic outlook of intercollegiate athletics as deeply problematic and unsustainable. The Knight Commission on Intercollegiate Athletics and a growing number of other organizations openly express their serious concerns over these trends and the outlook for the future. The economics of intercollegiate athletics, however, is only part of the sustainability equation. Questionable academic practices to ensure student athletes retain eligibility, inappropriate athletic department strategies for recruiting athletes, and periodic scandals that grab the nation's headlines and attention add to the challenges of universities as they seek to sustain intercollegiate athletics as they are currently structured and financed.

Costs of Intercollegiate Athletics

Getting an accurate assessment of the total cost for intercollegiate athletics is difficult. However, with the increasing transparency of the NCAA, it is possible to piece together a picture from various cost centers of the several conferences, conference subgroups, and clusters. The more revealing assessments of intercollegiate athletics finances have been carried out by investigative reporters for major news outlets, e.g., *The Washington Post, New York Times*, and others.

A *Washington Post* analysis based on NCAA data for the period 2004–2014 shows that the combined income of 48 athletic departments in college sports' wealthiest conferences nearly doubled, from $2.67 billion to $4.49 billion. Median earnings for the individual departments jumped from $52.9 million to $93.1 million. Notwithstanding the near-doubling of their incomes, more than half of the departments still ran a deficit in 2014 with two schools, Auburn and Rutgers, losing more money in 2014 than in 2004.[1]

Athletic directors are the biggest advocates for and defenders of the massive surge in athletic department incomes. Even those at money-losing departments strongly defend their spending as essential to keeping pace with competition. They claim their programs "benefit universities in ways that don't show on athletics financial statements." Their major and most frequently cited example is the media exposure for universities and the benefits of this exposure for increasing student applicants and fund-raising. Julie Hermann, Rutgers Athletic Director, commenting for the *Washington Post* article, states, "This is a competitive race among some of the biggest universities in this country to compete and achieve at the highest level."[2]

Critics of big-time athletics and their ballooning costs are growing both inside and outside the university. There is increasing recognition of the negative impact of these costs for students as well as their depressing influence on the academic mission of universities. The continuing failure of athletic programs to turn a profit or to even break even financially at some universities is "the result of the athletic director's decision to outspend income" and "evidence of systematic, wasteful spending" according to the *Washington Post* analysis.[3] David Ridpath, Ohio University business professor, studies intercollegiate athletics. His assessment is that college sports is a "very poorly run big business….It's frustrating to see universities, especially public ones, pleading poverty…and it is morally wrong for schools bringing in millions extra on athletics to continue to charge students and academics to support programs that, with a little bit of fiscal sense, could turn profits or at least break even."[4]

Critics, bloggers, news media, analysts, and a growing number of concerned individuals and organizations are asking, "Has spending become out of control for NCAA Athletics Departments?" One blogger among many, Brandon Birthed, writes in his May 22, 2017, blog, "As record revenues are brought in by college athletic departments, record losses are also being posted. How much money can be lost until the business model collapses? Will out of control spending be the end of college athletics?" For others, the more important question is: Will out-of-control spending by departments of athletics continue to inflict damaging wounds to the academic mission of universities?

The centerpiece of university athletic budgets is coaches' salaries. In most states—39 to be exact—coaches at state universities are the highest-paid public employees in the state.[5] *USA Today* compiles and reports salaries for university coaches. Their 2017 report for football coaches shows 76 (possibly 78) coaches receiving compensation from their university of $1.0 million or more (Table 8.1).[6]

Another dozen universities are poised and ready to spring for membership in the million-dollar coaches' club in the next year or two. At current rates of induction into the club, it is easy to anticipate 100 or more universities paying athletic coaches $1 million by 2020 and 200 by 2025. One must ask: Is this where taxpayers and tuition-paying students want their money to go?

The coaches' salary explosion began in the 1970s. Prior to that, football coaches were well paid with salaries generally in line with other

Table 8.1 Football coaches' compensation exceeding one million dollars

$11.0–11.9 M	1
$10.0–10.9 M	0
$9.0–9.9 M	0
$8.0–8.9 M	1
$7.0–7.9 M	1
$6.0–6.9 M	1
$5.0–5.9 M	4
$4.0–4.9 M	10
$3.0–3.9 M	19
$2.0–2.9 M	18
$1.0–1.9 M	21

administrators in leadership positions. Ohio State's Woody Hayes received $113,534 in 1951; Bear Bryant at Alabama earned $142,998 in 1958; Hayden Fry at SMU received $101,654 in 1962; and Bo Schembechler at Michigan, who once said, "No man is more important than The Team. No coach is more important than The Team," earned $135,127 in 1969.[7]

Why do university presidents, governing boards, state legislatures and governors permit and enable public universities to pay such inflated salaries at a time when the academic programs are cutting budgets, freezing faculty positions, eliminating programs, and hiring low-paid adjunct faculty to teach large sections of students, most of whom are borrowing money to pay tuition and mandatory athletic fees?

Athletics in the University Setting

One of the common university practices for meeting the athletic department budget is the imposition of mandatory student fees. University athletic programs levy large mandatory fees on university students—often without their knowledge or approval—to support the ballooning expenditures and budgets of athletic departments. These student fees combined with ticket sales, television revenue, and a host of other revenue sources have generated "big money" budgets and large cash flows. Because of the resources at their command, athletic directors and their departments—with the approval of their university presidents and governing boards—recruit coaches with million-dollar salaries, luxury-packed benefit packages, and product endorsement contracts that can exceed the collective faculty compensation of large academic departments or even whole colleges.

Athletic department revenues are also used to help ensure their student athletes retain eligibility. While the vast majority of student athletes meet their classes and compare favorably with other students in their academic performance, some academically challenged athletes are shielded from the rigors of more demanding disciplines, provided tutorial services and assistance, and given special treatment and benefits.

The influence, power, and resources of intercollegiate athletics on university campuses are also leveraged for construction of new or larger stadiums, high-end practice arenas, well-appointed locker rooms, luxurious interviewing lounges, and special recreation facilities dedicated to the sole use by athletes. Less visible to the campuses and public—unmeasured in cost but very real—is the time, effort, travel, and opportunity costs imposed by intercollegiate athletics on the university leadership and governing boards.

Of growing concern are the occasional but increasingly visible scandals that center on or involve intercollegiate athletics. The scope and scale of these scandals is evident in the sheer volume of media reports and investigations accumulating online. Some scandals go beyond shaving points and improper use of enhancing substances. University sports teams, coaches, and staff have been indicted for child sex abuse, paying sex workers to entertain recruits and athletes, and more. University reputations, careers, and lives have been negatively impacted or ruined by these scandals and illegal practices.

The pervasive and intrusive roles played by intercollegiate athletics, the outside controls imposed on universities by athletic conferences and their governing bodies, and the negative economic impact of athletics on students and taxpaying citizens call for a re-examination of institutional values and mission. For many observers, they call for real reform.

It is ironic that intercollegiate athletics has gained control over universities to such an extent that universities appear to be powerless to bring needed reform to their sports programs and deeply embedded sports cultures. Even influential higher education associations have been unable or unwilling to successfully confront the powers of intercollegiate athletics to bring about much-needed change and reforms. Even the prestigious and influential Knight Commission on Intercollegiate Athletics, with its mission of promoting reforms that support and strengthen the educational mission of college sports, has been limited to marginal improvements.

Financing Intercollegiate Sports and Mandatory Student Fees

Intercollegiate athletics is a huge and rapidly growing multi-billion-dollar industry. For anyone who follows college sports, it will not be surprising that the size of the intercollegiate athletics industry is increasing annually fueled by infusions of money from ticket sales, allocations from university funds, mandatory student fees, sales of sports wear and licensing commissions, event concession sales, television revenue, advertising, business and corporate sponsorships, donor contributions, and other sources. Revenue generation for intercollegiate athletics is very well organized and deeply embedded into nearly every part of higher education development and its broader infrastructure.

It is not something universities publicize, but information has been surfacing with greater frequency—largely through the efforts of students, student organizations, and the media—about the policies and practices of public universities of subsidizing intercollegiate sports programs with student tuition, mandatory fees, and tax dollars. These substantial subsidies—commonly in the tens of millions of dollars—constitute a serious problem and obstruction to the mission and quality of public higher education. These subsidies and expenditures at the vast majority of public universities come at the expense of students and their universities' *primary* mission, i.e., teaching, learning, research, and service.

The number of concrete, documented examples of how intercollegiate athletics is impacting universities and obstructing their efforts to achieve their education missions are too numerous to compile in a single book. However, a few such examples are cited to demonstrate the adverse economic impact of intercollegiate athletics on university campuses and provide insight into the need for genuine reform.

The *Texas Tribune* recently reported (May 1, 2018) "The cost of recruiting athletes has doubled at top Texas colleges. At some schools, students help foot the bill." Shannon Najmabadi and Daniel Levitt, reporters for *the Tribune*, describe the private jets, chartered cars and limousine services, visits to fancy restaurants, and other enticements that go into the annual athlete recruitment rituals. In the last ten years, recruitment costs have increased by 131% at eight Texas schools where the combined expenditures approached $10 million. Six of the eight Texas universities fund these expenses with subsidies from student fees and other institutional funds. Texas State's athletic program received $27.8 million in student fees and other institutional funds while the University of Texas San Antonio received $17.4 million from similar sources. At Texas State, the student subsidy is nearly $500 per year per student.[8]

A reporter for the *Buffalo News*, Jay Tokasz, identifies the problems and concerns felt by many in a 2015 article, "Small Crowds, Big Subsidy for UB Sports." In his focus on the University of Buffalo, Tokasz writes, "The price of pursuing athletic glory continues to climb at the University of Buffalo. And, footing much of the bill are students who don't suit up for games or even attend." Tokasz identifies the sources funding athletics at the University of Buffalo: Three-quarters of the UB athletic budget of $31.3 million—$24 million—was subsidized with students' fees, tuition, and tax dollars. This subsidy came at a time when academic budgets were frozen and there were shortages of faculty in some departments.[9]

This is an all-too-common story at public universities across the nation. A 2015 *Huffington Post/Chronicle of Higher Education* article describes the situation at Georgia State, a 32,000-student university, where over a recent five-year period, $90 million in student fees was allocated to cover the cost of football and other intercollegiate athletics. The authors of that story, Wolverton et al., describe the broader problem:

> A river of cash is flowing into college sports, financing a spending spree among elite universities that has sent coaches' salaries soaring and spurred discussions about whether athletes should be paid.[10]

The Huffington Post/Chronicle of Higher Education report that public universities have "pumped" more than $10.3 billion in mandatory student fees and other subsidies into their sports programs. This comes during a period when nearly all public colleges and universities are struggling with budget cuts and hiring freezes with no relief in sight. The informal, unspoken but clearly heard budget message to deans and department chairs is "do more with less," so we can continue to subsidize sports and intercollegiate athletics.

These mandatory student fees tend to increase, if not annually, every few years. Some of the increases outpace inflation and force students to take out ever-larger loans to pay for tuition and fees. The same article reports that "students who have the least interest in their college's sports teams are often required to pay the most to support them." Some large public universities are known to charge student athletic fees that exceed $1500 per year or $6000 over the course of four-year degree. Making matters even worse, most students are not aware of athletic fees or what such fees support but are, nevertheless, required to pay.[11]

Writing about universities in the Mid-America Conference (MAC), Nicholas Piotrowicz describes the "high cost of competing" for these Midwestern public institutions. His analysis reveals that the University of Toledo, my own institution,

> ...collected $10.5 million worth of mandatory student fees for the purpose of funding sports teams, while Bowling Green [State University] brought in $12.6 million. Across four years, recent graduates of UT gave about $2,000 each to fund the schools athletics...At Bowling Green, graduates give the department of athletics more than $3,200 each during a four-year undergraduate term...[12]

The MAC, a middle-range athletic conference, has 12 member universities including University of Toledo, Bowling Green State University, Eastern Michigan University, Central Michigan University, and Youngstown State University. Their combined expenditures for the members in 2005 were $184 million; ten years later, 2015, MAC university expenditures exceeded $326 million. Adjusting for inflation, Nicholas Piotrowicz's analysis reveals that MAC schools are spending more than $100 million per year above what they were spending just a decade ago.[13]

The growth and near-doubling of these athletic department budgets in the past ten years has resulted in ever-larger mandatory student fees and subsidization. The tragedy for students is that many, unfortunately, did not know they were paying the mandatory fees to support athletics; those who did know about the fee did not know how it was spent.

Rutgers professor, David Hughes, has studied the role and implications of these mandatory athletic fees. According to Hughes, these university subsidies for athletics undermine the university in two ways: They make it more expensive for students and weaken if not threaten the academic mission.[14] It is this growing expense that has driven ever-larger numbers of university students to ever-larger long-term student loans. The allocation and dedication of these large sums to athletics are funds that could have otherwise been used to strengthen academic programs or reduce the cost of education for students or both.

Many observers of the current trends are deeply concerned and argue correctly that students should not be charged a mandatory fee by their university for something they do not want, can't afford, have to borrow to pay for, and has nothing to do with their education. Reform of higher education must be accompanied by reform in intercollegiate athletics and how these programs are financed.

Student Athletes: Preferences, Pressures, and Price

Student athletes have not only a long history of preferential treatment but also a history of special challenges. These are topics of conversation on every campus and subjects of concern among sports writers, university faculty, team physicians, athletic interest groups, and others. How do we treat student athletes and is this treatment consistent with the mission and values of our colleges and universities?

Some campuses seek to blur or even hide the preferential treatment for athletes; others point to it as a matter of pride. Preferential treatment cuts across a range of instances and includes such concerns as university admission standards for athletically talented but academically deficient applicants, special assistance with study and class assignments, less-demanding academic programs at some universities, different grading standards, exclusive recreation facilities, and high-end residence halls and dining rooms dedicated to athletes. Other benefits include clothing, travel, media coverage, and, for some, celebrity status. These benefits packages and preferential treatment for student athletes are also causes for concern and have led to serious abuses in certain instances, some of which are picked up by various media outlets.

Gaining admission to selective colleges and universities can be challenging. Yet, an Associated Press review of NCAA data from 120 institutions with top-tier football programs shows "athletes enjoy strikingly better odds of having admission requirements bent on their behalf."[15] And the practice of special treatment in admissions was found to be "widespread" and "in every major conference." Tellingly, some universities—noted above—seek to keep these practices under wraps and out of the public eye; other universities such as University of Alabama and University of West Virginia are up-front with their preferential practices and even tout their flexibility as a strength in the interest of serving student athletes.

Stories abound about other forms of preferential treatment of athletes. Keeping athletes academically eligible to participate in intercollegiate sports is a demanding task for athletic departments. Academic "coaches" and special tutorial programs geared to assisting athletes with their studies, preparation for exams, and written assignments are commonplace at many universities. These services are funded by athletic departments and are free to athletes.

Spending on athletes is another area of preferential treatment that has gained attention in recent years. The *New York Times* has reported on the special treatment citing how universities spend "millions building new academic centers just for athletes."[16] Data available from NCAA document wide differences in university spending on athletes and non-athletes; the size of the difference in spending varies considerably by conference with some conferences spending 10–12 times as much on athletes as non-athletes. Such major differences in university spending on students based on their status as athletes are widely viewed as unfair and inappropriate. This is particularly true when it is considered that funds for these special services and perks for athletes are paid for, in part, through mandatory fees paid by non-athletes.

From the athletes' perspective, however, these services and perks are more than compensated for by their participation, hard work, hours of strenuous training, and sacrifice of discretionary time for the benefit of their university. Some are pushing back against the notion of preferential treatment as the following comments from athletes on Whisper, a "secret-sharing mobile app," demonstrate[17]:

> *I think we deserve it. I put in work during the week as a full-time student and athlete with a "job". We earn our scholarships just like other people. Tutoring? We have academic requirements to meet as well.*
> *You wake up at 5 to work out and condition for 2 hours then attend class and maintain a 3.5 to stay on the team then add 3-5 hours of practice a night and add 3 more hours if it [sic] game night. Then complain about our benefits.*
> *Are you freaking kidding me?! We work just as hard, hell, even harder than normal students. Why? Because we have practice and games to contend with and you don't!*
> *Yeah, they work their asses off! I only have a partial scholarship for the University of Florida for track and I've never worked so hard in my life! It's not just "playing a sport," it's a life style.*
> *Yes we do. I developed herniated disks from my sport. I think I deserve my free treatment I get.*

Athletes often feel the resentment or the negative attitudes of others on campus. A study of 538 college athletes sought to tap into the nature of relationships between athletes, fellow students, and faculty. The results confirm the feelings of athletes: a third report they were perceived negatively by professors. Nearly sixty percent (59.1%) felt they were perceived and treated negatively by other non-athlete students. Only fifteen percent reported positive perceptions. Athletes also report being "given a hard time" when requesting accommodations for athletic events and hearing negative stereotypical comments such as "dumb jock." They sense from others that they are being given undeserved benefits and privileges. One athlete commented: "If a professor knows you are an athlete, you are assumed to be stupid until you can prove otherwise."

The study reports attitudes and comments about athletes from professors. One professor is reported saying, "It's an easy test. Even athletes can pass." Another asked student athletes to stand on the first day of class and said, "These are the people who will probably drop this class." Other similar negative comments from professors were reported in the study. Athletes feel a "heavy burden…They are expected to be both successful in the academic as well as the athletic domain."[18]

Issues of fairness—for athletes and non-athletes—are topics on campuses across the nation, in major news and sports media, and among university leaders and policy makers. There is, in the minds of many, a "dramatic division" between the "haves" and "have-nots," between athletes and non-athletes. The system produces athletes who feel and believe they are being "exploited" and non-athletes who feel athletes have advantages they don't, advantages they are helping to pay for through their mandatory fees. The issue has been in need of resolution for decades without apparent progress or movement. But, as the sums of money flowing into intercollegiate athletics continue to grow, so does the pressure for resolving the complicated, controversial, and costly challenges that plague universities, athletic conferences, the NCAA, and, most importantly, athletes.

Can These Problems Be Solved and, If So, by Whom?

The most powerful entity in intercollegiate athletics is, of course, the NCAA. While it seeks to promote academics, well-being, and fairness in college sports, it has also been in the eye of the storm over its policies, practices, and perceived prejudices in the handling of an ever-growing host of scandals, controversial issues, and deeply engrained vested interests. The NCAA provides the governing structure for intercollegiate sports and manages issues relating to sports rules, championships, health and safety, matters impacting women in athletics, and opportunities for minorities.[19]

Many believe the solutions to the problems of intercollegiate athletics must, of necessity, come from the NCAA; others believe the NCAA

8 Intercollegiate Athletics: Challenge to the Academic Mission 117

is the *source* of many, if not most, of the problems in college sports. Notwithstanding the strengths of both perspectives, it is fair to argue that NCAA has been a conservative force that has, through its enormous power over college sports, maintained a status quo on many of the major issues and challenges facing intercollegiate athletics.

Is the NCAA capable of resolving the enormous challenges of university sports and intercollegiate athletics? It is unlikely in the extreme that the NCAA can resolve the major issues swirling around university athletics. Can the NCAA play a constructive role in resolving these issues? It seeks to play such a role, and many encourage it to assert its leadership in a more effective way. Will it succeed? The vested and financial interests represented in the governing bodies and committees of the Association make it difficult to be optimistic it will succeed.

The Knight Commission on Intercollegiate Athletics is also an important participant in the national dialogue on college and university sports. The mission and values of the Knight Commission read very much like those of the NCAA, e.g., health and safety of athletes, importance of education, integrity, and more. Formed in 1989 by John S. and James L. Knight, the Commission sought to advocate a reform agenda that would address the issues facing intercollegiate athletics at the time, i.e., low graduation rates of athletes and the highly visible scandals plaguing college sports. Membership in the Commission consists largely of current and former university presidents and chancellors, university trustees, former college athletes, and "thought leaders" from organizations engaged with higher education or athletics.[20]

The Commission can claim significant credit for nearly three decades of efforts, activities, and accomplishments. By all accounts, one of the Commission's signature accomplishments was their 1991 report, *Keeping Faith with the Student-Athlete: A New Model for Intercollegiate Athletics*. Described as a "roadmap for reform," the report was quickly accepted and supported by higher education leaders. The report advanced the notion of enhanced "presidential control directed toward academic integrity, financial integrity and independent certification." Within a decade, the NCAA had accepted and enacted most of the Commission's recommendations.

Subsequent Commission reports, *A Call to Action: Reconnecting College Sports and Higher Education* (2001) and *Restoring the Balance: Dollars, Values and the Future of College Sports* (2010) have continued their impact on the NCAA and university sports programs. Working from within the university sports culture and policy-making arena, the Commission seeks "achievable" reforms that will "create a foundation upon which future reforms can build."

Is the Knight Commission capable of bringing about the reforms needed to correct the imbalance between athletics and academics? Are they capable of ridding the system of the big money that influences and empowers athletics? Is the Commission capable of securing better alignment of the interests of college athletes, athletic conferences, and the NCAA with the mission and purposes of higher education? Most objective observers would give the Commission credit for making progress on many of the important issues and challenges facing intercollegiate athletics. However, the interlocking directorates and commissions that dominate college sports and their intimate relationships with member university presidents and trustees suffer the same vested interests that prevent the NCAA from genuine, sustainable reform. Overcoming these interests—largely financial—is desirable and needed but some argue is unrealistic and highly unlikely.

The level of frustration over the inability of established organizations to bring genuine reform to the major problems inherent in intercollegiate athletics has prompted others to seek alternative paths to reform. The Drake Group is one such organization. Founded in 1999, the Drake Group takes its motivation from "how the increased commercialization of big-money sports has been causing academic corruption in our universities." Leaders of the Drake Group call attention to the failure of universities—working within the policies of the NCAA and the influence of other vested interests—to rid university campuses of talented athletes who have little interest in nor the academic/learning background for serious university study. The Drake Group claims that the "United States is the only country where universities admit students who can't even read above grade school level so they can play basketball or football."[21]

The Drake Group envisions creating an atmosphere on college campuses "that encourages personal and intellectual growth for all students, and demands excellence and professional integrity from faculty charged with teaching." They seek greater accountability of trustees, administrators, and faculty regarding the quality of education received by college athletes. And, the Group seeks to be "a major lobby" for ensuring quality education for athletes.

Unlike the NCAA and the Knight Commission who are working to improve intercollegiate athletics from within, the Drake Group approaches the deeply embedded problems working from outside the athletic establishment. In their work, they seek to engage governors, state legislatures, the US Department of Education, and concerned citizens to take action. They are calling on universities to be more transparent "so the public can see" what they are actually doing in athletics. They want the public to have a clear picture of "how bad" it has become.[22]

Conclusions

Intercollegiate athletics is a prime example of how public higher education is losing its sense of purpose and direction when students are required to pay mandatory fees to support athletic programs with borrowed funds they will be repaying with interest for years or decades; when coaches are paid ten, twenty or thirty times as much as full professors; when academic department budgets are frozen at the same time athletic budgets are growing rapidly; when admission criteria are bent or sometimes broken to admit students who are academically unqualified but happen to be good athletes; when athletes are funded at levels ten to twelve times the funding of non-athlete students; and when attempts at reform continue decade after decade with little or no significant change in the fundamental structural relationship between athletics and their host universities.

James L. Shulman and William G. Bowen, in their comprehensive, revealing, and critical analysis of intercollegiate athletics, *The Game of Life: College Sports and Educational Values* (2001), come to the same conclusion. They write:

Failure to see where the intensification of athletic programs is taking us, and to adjust expectations could have the unintended consequence of allowing intercollegiate athletics to become less and less relevant to the educational experiences of most students and more and more at odds with the core missions of the institutions themselves. The objective... should be to strengthen the links between athletics and the educational missions of colleges and universities—to reinvigorate an aspect of college life that deserves to be celebrated for its positive contributions, not condemned for its excesses or criticized for its conflicts with educational values.[23]

The relationship between athletics and universities is a malfunctioning coexistence that, at least in its current configuration, is another example that the public higher education paradigm is broken and may not be sustainable in its present form. In the big picture, intercollegiate athletics at all but a few public universities adds to students' cost and detracts from the educational quality of academic programs they receive.

References

1. Will Hobson and Steven Rich, "Playing in the Red," *Washington Post* (November 23, 2015).
2. Ibid.
3. Ibid.
4. Ibid.
5. Cork Gaines, "The Highest-Paid Public Employee in 39 States Is Either a Football or Men's Basketball Coach," *Business Insider* (September 22, 2016).
6. Steve Berkowitz, Christopher Schnaars, and Sean Dougherty, "NCAA Salaries," *Sports* (usatoday.com, 2017).
7. Paul Campos, "A Brief History of College Football Coaching Salaries in the Context of the New Gilded Age," *Lawyers, Guns and Money* (December 20, 2014).
8. Shannon Najmabadi and Daniel Levitt, "The Cost of Recruiting Athletes Has Doubled at Top Texas Colleges. At Some Schools the Students Help Foot the Bill," *The Texas Tribune* (May 1, 2018).

9. Jay Tokasz, "Small Crowds Big Subsidy for UB Sports," *The Buffalo News* (November 29, 2015).
10. Brad Wolverton, Ben Hallman, Shane Shifflett, and Sandhya Kambhampati, "Sports at Any Cost: How College Students Are Bankrolling the Athletics Arms Race," *The Huffington Post/Chronicle of Higher Education* (November 15, 2015).
11. Ibid.
12. Nicholas Piotrowicz, "MAC Schools Cost of Athletics Up 75% Over Last 10 Years," *The Blade* (June 5, 2016).
13. Ibid.
14. Bryan Alexander, *How Public Universities Support Athletics—and Students—Badly* (November 16, 2015).
15. Associated Press, *Report: Exemptions Benefit Athletes* (December 30, 2009).
16. Tyler Kingkade, "These College Athletes Say They Deserve Special Treatment," *Huffington Post* (September 2, 2004).
17. Ibid.
18. Elizabeth Tovar, *Faculty Perceptions of Division I Male Student-Athletes: The Relationship Between Student-Athlete Contact, Athletic Department Involvement and Perceptions of Intercollegiate Athletics* (Ph.D. dissertation, University of Kansas, no date).
19. NCAA, *Official Website*.
20. Knight Commission, *Official Website*.
21. The Drake Group, *Official Website*.
22. Ibid.
23. James L. Shulman and William G. Bowen, *The Game of Life: College Sports and Educational Values* (Princeton and Oxford: Princeton University Press, 2001), 309.

9

Presidential Selection, Salaries, and Moral Leadership

I will admit a little bias, but I think many would agree that the position of college or university president is one of the most respected, prestigious roles in any community. It is a high honor to be selected president of an institution of higher education. Most institutions have long histories dating back many decades and can boast of a legacy that includes being among the city's or region's largest employers; alma mater to many of the community's leading citizens, professionals, and business owners; center of social life and entertainment; sponsor of the major sports teams; and being a major economic driver for the area. College and university presidents are entrusted with this legacy and the responsibility to strengthen the role their institution plays in the community, region, and state. There are few, if any, positions of greater importance in any community.

The American Council on Education (ACE) has had a long-standing interest in the presidency. Looking back, their 2012 *American College President Study* report revealed that in 1986, the typical president was a white male in his 50s, married with children, Protestant, held a doctorate in education, and had served in his current position for six years. Twenty-five years later, the profile had changed but not significantly

© The Author(s) 2019
D. M. Johnson, *The Uncertain Future of American Public Higher Education*,
https://doi.org/10.1007/978-3-030-01794-1_9

with the exception of age and gender. For example, in 1986 the average age of college and university presidents was 52; by 2011, it was 61. In fact, in 1986 just 13% of presidents were over the age of 60: By 2011, 58% of presidents were in the over-60 cohort. This may have been the most significant change in the demographic makeup of the presidency in the twenty-five-year period.[1]

Racial diversity of college presidents increased slightly in the twenty-five years between 1986 and 2011 from 8 to 13%. However, when comparing data from 2006 and 2011, racial diversity actually declined from 14 to 13%. There was, however, some headway in gender diversity during this twenty-five-year period. In 1986, just 10% of college presidents were women: By 2011, 26% of institutional leaders were female.[2]

One of the important characteristics of the university presidency is the professional background, experience, and career path that lead to this position. The ACE study found that most presidents spent their entire careers in higher education; in fact, more than half of the presidents never worked outside higher education. The largest percentage had been chief academic officers prior to their presidencies, and three-quarters served as full-time faculty members at some point in their career.

By 2017, there were modest changes in the characteristics of those occupying the presidency, but the position continued to be largely held by white males with doctoral degrees in their early 60s. The percentage of women in presidencies increased to 30%, up four percentage points in the previous five years. The percentage of minority presidents also increased by four percentage points from 13% in 2011 to 17% in 2016. Perhaps even more significant during this period of rapid change, the most common road to the presidency continued to be the traditional route of academic affairs (43%). There is, however, some evidence that this may be changing.[3]

The college and university president is, by almost any measure, the most influential and important role in higher education. It is a role that will take on even greater importance in the challenging era ahead. Charting the future for institutions of higher education requires a broad, holistic perspective that embraces the economic, political, social, demographic, and educational forces impacting our colleges and universities as well as the powerful forces of change underway in each of these spheres. Understanding these forces and charting a course of action for our institutions of higher education are necessary but not sufficient qualities for successful future presidents. Persons selected to fill these critically important roles must possess superb leadership skills that inspire trust, confidence, and a willingness of the institutions' many constituents to follow in pursuit of its mission.

College and university presidents of the future will need more than an excellent academic pedigree to lead their institutions; indeed, it may be that the academic qualities on which we based our selection of presidents in the past are no longer the qualities most needed for these complex and challenging roles in the future. In-depth knowledge of an academic discipline, research in that field, and years of teaching, while important and helpful, are not the most important qualifications for leading complex organizations. Even the experience of climbing the academic administration ladder—department chair, dean, provost, and other administrative posts—while helpful is insufficient preparation for meeting the leadership responsibilities and challenges faced by college and university presidents.

Most of the positions on the academic ladder labeled "administration" are, in reality, middle management roles. Professors recruited to or who seek to fill these roles would, likely, take exception to being called "managers," but a careful reading of their duties and responsibilities leaves no question as to their managerial character. Presidents must understand academic management, but they must also be accomplished leaders. They must see the "big picture" and the path forward, but even with that vision, they must also be able to motivate the many constituencies of the college or university to accept the need for change and offer informed strategies for making needed changes.

It is most unfortunate and ironic that the one position in academia that can help address the major challenges and looming crises in higher education is also one that is part of the mix of challenging, problematic issues, i.e., the college and university presidency. Two major challenges involving the presidency have evolved over the past few decades: First is the changing context and demands of the presidency and the way in which presidents are chosen to address these demands. The second is a problem that has been created by trustees and continues to grow, i.e., presidential compensation, benefits, and perks.

Presidential Selection: Succession Planning Needed

Selection of a president is, without doubt, the single most important task of a college or university governing board. Choosing institutional leaders cannot be surpassed in importance by any other decision. Yet, today, there are increasingly serious questions and growing concerns about the collective efficacy of these decisions and the processes that proceed them and lead to presidential appointments. Why is that and what's happening?

Turnover among college and university presidents has been increasing and is likely to increase in future years if for no other reason than the aging of current incumbents. If presidential turnover increases, it could easily become one of those challenges confronting American higher education that if not adequately addressed could soon become a serious problem and concern. For some colleges and universities, it is already a serious concern.

Failed presidencies are no longer a rarity and have, in fact, become the subject for dissertations, papers, journal articles, and even books. The growing complexities of the institutions combined with continuing reductions in state subsidy and support have, for many colleges and universities, created a near-perfect storm where seasoned, well-prepared, effective leadership is essential but frequently missing. The presidential selection process itself is often a factor in failed presidencies when the process does not produce appropriate or qualified candidates.

The problem most universities and their trustees fail to see or refuse to confront is the nature of the processes by which presidents and leadership teams are selected. Presidential selection *traditions* are deeply ingrained in the academic culture, and these traditions are increasingly failing the institutions and damaging or limiting our system of higher education at a time strong, well-informed, proactive leadership is most needed. Unfortunately, the vast majority of universities and colleges do not have anything that even remotely resembles succession planning for selecting presidents apart from these traditions. The current, traditional process is flawed, some say broken, and new, better thinking and planning is required to prevent the problem of presidential selection from getting worse and further weakening American higher education.

The only significant change in the presidential selection process in the past quarter century has been the addition of outside consultants. Interestingly, the primary function of outside consultants, in most instances, is to help ensure that the traditional approach is followed, that all bases of that approach are touched to ensure the inclusion of key stakeholders in the process, and, finally, that the trustees are presented with a small group of "qualified" candidates from whom they pick the one, hopefully, that is the "best fit."

The traditional approach to presidential selection is also costly in terms of real costs, opportunity costs, time, and outcomes. More problematic, the selection process frequently fails to produce the right mix of knowledgeable and experienced candidates for the institution and role. Since these presidential searches are almost always *national* searches, it usually results in bringing in a new president from the "outside" who knows very little or nothing about the institution, its history, or the important issues facing the campus. Consequently, even the most qualified new presidents need time—a year or more—to learn enough about the institution and history of the issues to actually begin making informed decisions and leading with confidence.

Given the importance of presidential appointments, it is surprising, puzzling, and even shocking that colleges and universities have not embraced succession planning. In fact, succession planning for university presidents and senior officers is almost nonexistent in higher education. It is ironic inasmuch as our institutions are well known for strategic planning and devote considerable time, effort, and other resources to the various planning projects commonly underway on most campuses. But the selection of presidents, provosts, vice-presidents, and deans almost always starts from scratch with a national or international search soliciting expressions of interest, applications, and nominations without much more than a job description and institutional profile to go with it.

Several higher education associations and a few universities sponsor "schools" for new presidents and other leadership positions. They are helpful and contribute to the preparation of new presidents by providing an introduction to their new roles and responsibilities, e.g., fund-raising, working with faculty and faculty senates, the role and responsibility of boards, budgeting, alumni, and other relevant topics. The value of these schools for many new presidents is putting these nominal roles and responsibilities into the context and framework of the position. Programs and schools for new presidents are a bit of a reality check for some. The other value, I found in my experience, was in the opportunity for networking with others who were also moving into presidencies; these relationships proved useful over time.

I can recall quite vividly my frame of mind when I first arrived on campus to assume the presidency of a large, Midwestern, metropolitan university. Driving up to the campus and finding my assigned parking place, I recognized that everyone I would meet for the next several weeks or months knew more about the university than I knew, but I had the responsibility for decision-making and leading the campus. Every issue and every decision had a history and constituents, frequently with differing points of view. I quickly learned that for every issue there were often several different camps that had their own perspectives and points of view; for every dollar in the budget, there were multiple claims, and for every hour of my day, there were those who felt entitled to it.

Settling in, getting up to speed on the countless issues; developing working relationships with the administrative leadership; gaining an understanding of the various, sometimes conflictive positions of trustees on finance, policy, and personnel matters; and meeting the many community influentials, civic leaders, and public officials that have a say— or believe they should have a say—in university matters take months and often years. The challenge and burden of grasping and "getting out in front" of these issues fall squarely on the new president. We jokingly called this "drinking from a firehose." Not only does the new president find this transition period challenging and sometimes difficult, but also the whole university pays a price by the need to slow things down for a period of time until the new president gets up to speed on issues that require his or her decision and action.

The case for succession planning for college and university presidents and other senior officials cannot be stronger. Selecting leaders for some of our most important and complex institutions should not be left to luck, the role of the dice or even traditional processes. I've heard trustees and others say, commenting about their new president, "We were really *lucky* to get her or him." But there are often other common expressions that are less positive about presidential searches: "It wasn't a very strong pool of candidates." "I'm not sure our executive search firm was right for us." "Our best candidate was lost to another university at the last minute." "We had to go to our second choice because we couldn't get faculty (or trustee) agreement on our first choice." Or, "We should have started over."

Succession planning also allows governing boards and major stakeholders to more effectively provide for and ensure desired continuity as well as needed change through the selection of a new president. One of the classic failures of many new presidents is launching their new administration without sufficient regard for "what work," past advances, major initiatives currently underway, and earlier visions for the university that may still hold great promise. Some new presidents, unfortunately, take the reins and forge a totally new path that ignores earlier goals, investments, and strategies. All too often this approach leaves faculty and staff confused or worse, apathetic or even hostile to the new vision and programs of the new president. Succession planning, with its emphasis on desired continuity as well as needed change, offers greater promise for successful presidential searches.

The weaknesses of the long-standing, traditional approach to presidential searches are increasingly recognized and sources of growing concern. Joel Trachtenberg, President Emeritus, George Washington University and author of a book on failed presidencies, advises governing boards to "get their act together."[4] Some of these searches turn into a "train wreck" for all parties with the end result weakening the institution as well as all of higher education. The challenges and opportunities for higher education in the USA have never been greater, but without the right leadership, the opportunities are lost or never seized and the resulting challenges are often disappointing or overwhelming for the whole institution.

The Association of Governing Boards of Universities and Colleges (AGB) is among those taking the lead on declaring the need for succession planning in higher education and presidential searches. They point out that unlike other complex organizations, higher education has not embraced succession planning. Locked in an outmoded, ineffective tradition for selecting presidents and other leaders, universities have frequently failed to live up to their potential and, more seriously, failed to adapt to the rapid changes and challenges impacting higher education. That needs to change; AGB now makes the case that "presidential succession planning and systematic leadership development are important tools for ensuring continued strong leadership of colleges and universities and the success of long-term institutional goals."

AGB identifies three major problems on the horizon for the presidency that are making succession planning particularly important: (1) The aging of current presidents will lead to unprecedented turnover in the next ten years. The ACE reports that the average age of sitting presidents is 61.7 years; (2) the same turnover is expected among chief academic officers who have traditionally filled the pipeline to the academic presidency; and (3) the demand for top presidential candidates will result in intense competition among institutions.[5]

In addition to the AGB list of problems, there are significant problems in diversifying the top leadership positions in higher education, a growing reluctance among provosts to seek university presidencies, and a serious lack of awareness from governing boards that the traditional presidential selection process is no longer adequate. The result is the perpetuation of a very traditional selection process that has serious and growing limitations for presidential searches.

A 2008 survey of presidents and trustees suggests that there may be "a growing alarm" among some over the lack of succession planning and preparation for presidential selection. The results of the survey also suggest openness to succession planning. However, the description that succession planning is taking hold in higher education is misleading and, in all likelihood, reflects the views of the few—eight percent—who responded to the survey.[6]

Where succession planning is occurring, the most common form is identifying and nurturing internal leaders. Even here, however, the survey shows there is a "negative perception of proactively identifying successors." There is also the view that "all positions require an open, public search." Succession planning is further challenged by the commitment to diversity; survey results suggest that this may be one of the "biggest challenges."[7]

Respondents to the survey also expressed concern that the philosophy of shared governance represents a major challenge to succession planning. The survey found that succession planning, from the respondents' perspective, should be transparent, participatory, and intentional. Perhaps the most important finding from this 2008 survey was "succession planning in higher education requires new thinking and cultural change, but is overdue."[8]

The tradition-bound practices and protocols for selecting university and college presidents and others in key leadership positions tend to ignore the importance of institutional history and policy memory in favor of new, outside leaders uncontaminated by institutional politics or even knowledge of the major issues. Understanding the subtle nuances of university histories, policy and personnel decisions can be and frequently are important elements that contribute to the avoidance of major mistakes and to successful leadership. Although the major challenges facing higher education are those associated with the rapid changes taking place in our society, economy, and culture, there are also major challenges associated with maintaining continuity in the mission, core values, and functions of our colleges and universities that continue to be relevant.

More than ever, institutions of higher education need to challenge the adequacy of past traditions in the selection of presidents and university leaders and embrace the concept and values of succession planning. Governors should encourage greater adoption of succession planning and boards of trustees, as good stewards, owe it to their institutions to pursue more effective models and processes for selecting presidents and other campus leaders.

Presidential Salaries

In addition to all of the challenges facing higher education is another "sacred cow" that is beginning to draw attention, i.e., presidential salaries. As a former university president, I've watched this issue surface during the past decade which, in the larger context, includes the growing student loan crisis, shrinking resources for student scholarships and increasing numbers of adjunct and part-time faculty due to the lack of funds to hire regular, full-time faculty, to mention just a few.

An important 2014 study by the Institute for Policy Studies sheds some light on the issue. From 2009 to 2012, executive pay at public research universities increased by 14% to an average of $544,554. The highest-paying universities (Ohio State, Penn State, University of Minnesota, University of Michigan, and University of Washington) averaged close to million-dollar presidential salaries $974,006.[9] And that was five years ago!

The Chronicle of Higher Education regularly publishes the salaries of university presidents. According to *the Chronicle* (2017), chief executives of 59 private colleges and seven public universities took home more than $1 million in total compensation in 2015.[10] NPR's Amy Kamenetz, writing about the new information, described it as "eye-popping" and "a record."[11] *The Chronicle* also reported that the "three highest paid public university leaders each took home more than $1,000,000 last fiscal year." Presidential compensation in private universities skyrocketed to a record high with several presidents receiving paychecks surpassing $3,000,000 and some reaching $5,000,000. These salaries often do not include other significant benefits in their compensation packages such as deferred compensation, housing, cars, club memberships, first-class air travel, and expense accounts that are often nearly unlimited. Many provide compensation for spouses of presidents who, in many if not most instances, devote time and effort to university activities.[12]

Public universities claim they have to pay these salaries to remain competitive with private universities that pay even higher salaries. Michael Crow, President of Arizona State University, took home the largest salary of public university presidents, $1,554,058. The University of Texas System reports three officials with million-dollar salaries. While the average salary for public university presidents is nearing $500,000, many have surpassed that and are approaching those in the million-dollar range. These salaries are being offered at a time when many universities claim they lack funds for needed faculty positions and are seeking more part-time and adjunct faculty to fill the positions of regular faculty. William Tierney, professor at the University of Southern California, who studies university leadership, has expressed concern over the sources of funding for presidential compensation, particularly funds taken from university foundations. He argues "There should be greater oversight that needs to come from state legislatures."[13]

These million-dollar-plus salaries are also attracting the concern and attention of Congress. Proposals in both the US House and Senate have called for tax-exempt organizations to pay a 20% excise tax on the salaries of their five top earners who have compensation in excess of $1 million, i.e., the "millionaires' club." Texas officials, responding to criticism, claim that these million-dollar salaries are "reasonable and justified."[14]

No one doubts the difficulty, complexity, or the important responsibilities that come with these positions. Yet, it is difficult to understand how the duties of these university presidents surpass those of the President of the USA whose salary, set by Congress, is $400,000. True, the US President is furnished with a very nice house, a very special plane, and other amenities. But to think that some universities pay their presidents twice or three times the salary of the US President certainly raises questions in this era of tight budgets, high tuitions, mandatory fees, record-breaking student loans and indebtedness, shortages of full-time faculty, deferred maintenance on campuses, and a host of other costly challenges.

The lavishness of high presidential salaries and compensation packages at a time other areas of the university are suffering faculty and personnel cutbacks and budget cuts is indicative of poor judgment on the part of university governing boards and their compensation committees. And, recognizing that these salaries are paid for in most cases with revenue derived from student tuition and tax dollars as well as donor contributions leaves conscientious observers of higher education with the view that some governing boards fail to grasp the sad irony of this picture.

For these and other observers of public higher education, extreme salaries are still another reason for calling for a new approach that finds greater balance and linkage between the expenditures we place on students, their families, and taxpayers and the compensation of university leaders. It may well be that the presidents themselves will need to lead in this area, insisting that their own salaries remain in proper context. Some have actually done so. The Deloitte's Center for Higher Education Excellence foresees such action: "As higher education faces demographic and financial challenges in the decade ahead, the role and expectations of the college president are also undergoing substantial change…"[15] Expectations for million-dollar compensation packages should be among those that undergo change.

The argument that public universities must pay these million-dollar salaries to compete with private universities is spurious, not true nor convincing. Throughout every city and state, there are nonprofit organizations that fall far short of their neighboring private corporations with respect to CEO compensation. Private, for-profit corporations and public, nonprofit universities draw on talent from two very different sectors, each understanding the values, compensation philosophies, and differences of the two sectors. Those pursuing careers and opportunities to serve in the nonprofit sector are seldom, motivated by salary. Those who are motivated by compensation know the limits of the public sector, and if salaries in that sector are not adequate, they have the choice to pursue career opportunities in the private sector, or even other professions.

Presidential Moral Leadership

The increasing complexity of issues and challenges facing higher education and problems that often go to the heart of collegiate and community values requires *every* college and university campus to have strong moral leadership. The reasons for this assertion are clear to every university leader. Every day, twenty-four–seven, presents leaders of our institutions of higher education a cacophony of important decisions, many of which have buried beneath the surface moral issues that touch the lives of students, faculty, staff, fellow administrators, alumni, and entire communities and beyond. Every day, decisions by the president and campus leaders strengthen and reinforce the brand and image of the institution or do damage to the most important asset of any college or university, its reputation as an honorable institution.

Institutions and their leaders are not only responsible for their own judgment and decisions, but also vulnerable to the consequences of bad judgment and poor decisions by nearly anyone on campus. Improper behavior or poor judgment displayed any place on campus can, potentially, work its way up the administrative chain to the president and even the board of trustees. When these events occur—and they occur on every campus every year—the moral leadership of the institution is challenged and will often determine the outcome.

One of the great, untold stories on nearly every American college or university campus is how the president and administration, on a daily basis, pass the many tests and challenges to their moral leadership. These stories rarely find their way to the local media and may be known by only a few. Unfortunately, the failures almost always get told, often on the front page of the local newspaper, and some become statewide or even national scandals, the effects of which are felt for years, even decades. The seriousness of some scandals brings institutional scars that never quite go away.

The Washington Post collected and ran the stories of these failures with the headline: *Eight Scandals That Ended College Presidencies.* In each case, the institutions gained unfavorable national attention (Table 9.1).[16]

The number and nature of these scandals became a cloud over all of higher education across the nation. Stories about universities and their leaders started popping up around the country citing a variety of incidents. After noticing a series of university presidents "who had gotten the ax," Stephen Joel Trachtenberg and colleagues Gerald Kauvar and Grady Bogue began looking into these incidents. What they discovered

Table 9.1 Media coverage of university failures

University of Illinois	Admissions scandal
University of Colorado	Recruiting scandal
American University	Expense account scandal
St. Bonaventure	NCAA scandal
Eastern Michigan University	Crime scandal
UC Santa Cruz	Suicide
Hillsdale College	Sex scandal and suicide
Montgomery College	Expense account scandal

was surprising. In the period 2009–2010, 50 college presidents "left or were pushed out before the end of their first contract period."[17]

The causes of their terminations were "ethical lapses, poor interpersonal skills, inability to lead key constituencies, difficulty adapting, failure to meet financial objectives and board shortcomings." Every president understands how these things—these failures—can and do happen. The potential for such happenings is present in multiple daily decisions. Trachtenberg and his colleagues also found "many presidential collapses are hidden by tight-lipped and embarrassed board members and presidents—as well as non-disclosure agreements." When ethical lapses or failures occur, the institutions' public relations machinery swings into action to prevent public disclosures or, if that is not possible, couch the story in the best way possible to protect the institution. Trachtenberg observes: "You can't learn anything from that."[18]

For university presidents and their administrative teams and trustees, moral leadership is a different but indispensable form of leadership. The Global Ethics Network describes moral leadership as leadership that aspires to serve more than being followed. Moral leadership is about developing the capacities of others. It is characterized by a "deep sense of ethics," "driven by core ideals," and "motivated by the pursuit of a higher purpose." Okra Chukwuebuka Zeal writing in the Global Ethics Network captures the essence of moral leadership in the following:

> First of all, Moral Leaders know how to manage themselves, how to temper their egos and how to act with nobility and rectitude. They are visionary and affect personal change. Moral Leaders also have a highly developed sense of emotional intelligence and master key social skills.

They work to overcome obstacles and are skilled at the art of consultation. They build consensus, navigate diversity and establish unity. Moral Leaders are the conscience (i.e., moral compass) of an enterprise or organization and the glue that holds it together.[19]

Every college, university, and institution of higher education needs this kind of leadership.

In his classic work, *Good to Great*, Jim Collins describes this kind of leadership as "Level 5 Leadership." Collins describes Level 5 leaders as "ambitious first and foremost for the company…set up their successors for even greater success in the next generation…display compelling modesty, are self-effacing…display a workmanlike diligence—more plow horse than show horse…When things go poorly, they look in the mirror and take responsibility…" Collins goes on to observe that "One of the most damaging trends in recent history is the tendency (especially by boards of directors) to select dazzling, celebrity leaders and to de-select potential Level 5 leaders."[20]

More than any other quality, moral leadership must find its way into every college and university through the board of trustees, president, and senior administrative team. The cornerstone of moral leadership is trust: To be trusted, institution leaders must be trustworthy. Worthiness is won daily through the decisions routinely made by trustees, presidents, and other campus leaders. In the case of public universities, it is won through the appointments made to the boards of trustees by the governor, presidential appointments made by boards of trustees, and appointments made to senior leadership positions by the president. The subject of moral leadership should also find its way onto the agendas of board retreats, cabinet meetings, and administrative councils. The "values statements" published by every institution of higher education should be imprinted in places where they can serve as a daily reminder of what our colleges and universities stand for.

The need for moral leadership is not limited only to crises and scandals but extends to policy matters and budget decisions. Decision-makers—trustees, presidents, provosts, and deans—must keep in mind the impact of every decision, every allocation, and every compensation package on the students they serve. Many of these decisions are very difficult. In my own case, when a particularly difficult budget decision or expenditure request would come across my desk for approval, I would sometimes stop and ask how my dad—a hardworking, blue-collar, high-school graduate and taxpayer—would feel about spending his tax dollars or tuition revenue for this. I felt a sense of guidance through this exercise that often helped in these difficult calls.

Conclusion

The leadership opportunities that come with the Office of President are unlimited. Although the daily challenges, problems, and difficulties faced by college and university presidents are real and often surpass in complexity those in other sectors, the opportunities to make a positive difference in the lives of students and those in the campus community are real and regularly surpass such opportunities CEOs in other sectors may have. However, to realize these opportunities fully, it is important for university leaders to embrace the moral dimension in their leadership. This means making the education, welfare, and safety of students the number-one priority in every decision and action. The daily, routine demands of the Office of President must not cause the occupants to lose sight of the larger leadership role—the moral leadership role—that our campuses and communities need and expect.

The moral leadership of colleges and universities reaches far beyond the campus and impacts all of our nation's institutions of higher education. If public opinion about higher education has any significance, there is a big job ahead for the leaders of these institutions. A recent Gallup poll revealed that 56% of Americans said they had "some or very little" confidence in higher education. This perception is bipartisan: 67% of Republicans distrust colleges and universities as do 43% of Democrats.[21]

The nation's higher education leaders need a strategy to address this dramatic loss of confidence witnessed by our colleges and universities in recent decades. Although there are many views on how to regain the public's trust in higher education, three such strategies are offered by Jonathan Zimmerman, education historian at University of

Pennsylvania.[22] They are included here in support of the need for strategic leadership on this important issue.

1. Declare a moratorium on salary increases for university presidents.
2. Declare a second moratorium on the construction of nonacademic facilities.
3. Guarantee freedom of speech.

It strikes me that this would be a good starting point.

References

1. American Council on Education in partnership with TIAA, *The American College President Study 2017.*
2. Ibid.
3. Ibid.
4. Joel Trachtenberg, Gerald Kauvar, and Grady Bogue, *Presidencies Derailed: Why University Leaders Fail and How to Prevent It* (Baltimore: The Johns Hopkins University Press, 2013).
5. Association of Governing Boards, *Presidential Succession Planning*, agb.org.
6. Witt/Kieffer, *Succession Planning Takes Hold in Higher Education*, www.wittkieffer.com.
7. Ibid.
8. Ibid.
9. Institute for Policy Studies, *The One Percent at State U: How Public University Presidents Profit from Rising Student Debt and Low Wage Faculty Labor* (May 21, 2014).
10. Dan Bauman, Tyler Davis, Ben Myers, and Brian O'Leary, "Executive Compensation at Private and Public Colleges, Chronicle of Higher Education," (December 10, 2017).
11. Amy Kamenetz, *More College Presidents Join the Millionaires Club* (NPR, December 13, 2017).
12. *Chronicle of Higher Education*, ibid.
13. *Forbes* (July 17, 2017).
14. Associated Press, *Study Finds Pay for Public College Presidents Up 5.3 Percent* (June 28, 2017).

15. Jason Maderer, "Nationwide Wave of Change Coming to Role of College and University Presidents," *Georgia Tech News Center* (April 19, 2017).
16. Daniel de Vise, "Eight Scandals That Ended College Presidencies," *Washington Post* (November 21, 2011).
17. Joel Trachtenberg et al., ibid.
18. Ry Rivard, "Avoiding Disastrous Presidencies," *Inside Higher Ed* (October 4, 2013).
19. Okorie Chukwuebuka Zeal, "What Moral Leadership Means to Me," *Global Ethics Network* (January 1, 2014).
20. Jim Collins, *Good to Great: Why Some Companies Make the Leap and Others Don't* (New York: Harper Collins, 2001).
21. Doug Lederman, "Is Higher Education Really Losing the Public?," *Inside Higher Ed* (December 15, 2017).
22. Jonathan Zimmerman, "Three Ways Colleges and Universities Can Earn Back America's Receding Trust," *The Inquirer* (December 28, 2017).

10

Student Demographics: The Coming Changes and Challenges for Higher Education

The famous quotation, "Demography is destiny," often attributed to the father of sociology, Auguste Comte, is one that should be on the minds of education policy makers and university leaders. The lifeblood of our colleges and universities has been and continues to be the steady stream of young adults, most of whom are between the ages of 18 and 24, who come from families with the means and motivation to help their sons and daughters with the ever-rising cost of higher education. This steady and often growing stream of students has been the source of increasing enrollments, new universities, the opening of branch campuses, new residence halls, new classrooms, new academic degree programs, stadiums, recreation centers, and more.

But that growth may be coming to an end. The stream of students is shrinking and for some institutions drying up. The growth model for colleges and universities based on ever-increasing enrollments will no longer apply to most institutions. The assumption made by most institutions that they would continue to get "their share" of the increasing student population is unrealistic in a shrinking student market. This is new territory. Demographers and other observers of our nation's population are now sounding an alert to significant changes in the number

© The Author(s) 2019
D. M. Johnson, *The Uncertain Future of American Public Higher Education*,
https://doi.org/10.1007/978-3-030-01794-1_10

and composition of students in the pipeline that could bring equally significant economic challenges or even crises for many colleges and universities.

One of the themes of this book is the *uncertain future* for higher education. However, in this one area—demography—there are some *certainties* that are definitely going to impact higher education in the USA. The results of that impact, however, leave us again with great uncertainties. We have highly detailed demographic data from the US Census and population studies that tell us in fairly precise numbers the size of the college-going populations in future years. We know the college-going rates for the subgroups in the population. Using these and other demographic tools, we can forecast fairly accurately what is going to happen and the changes we are going to encounter. What are these demographic changes, and are universities and colleges prepared for their impact?

Perhaps the most significant demographic fact is the number of high school graduates of both public and private high schools is going to be stagnant for the near future with a very modest increase in 2024–2025. Beyond that, the number of high school graduates decreases for the next half decade. These projections are based on the work of the Western Interstate Commission for Higher Education (WICHE). WICHE has been producing projections of high school graduates for nearly 40 years. Their publication, *Knocking at the College Door: Projections of High School Graduates,* portrays the next decade of college admissions as one of increased competition, particularly for those outside the highly ranked, prestigious universities.[1]

WICHE's latest projections in December 2016 indicate that the number of graduates in each graduating class will average around 3.4 million through 2023 before peaking at 3.56 million prior to 2026. At the same time, the number of high school graduates from private religious and nonsectarian schools is projected to decline. From 2027 through the early 2030s, the number of high school graduates will be fewer than the number recorded in 2013.[2] During this period of demographic doldrums with little or no growth in the college-age population, it should be anticipated that a significant number of colleges and universities will experience slight to modest decreases in applications and enrollment. Institutions that are largely dependent on tuition income will find the next decade even more challenging than past decades.

In addition to the lack of growth in the number of high school graduates will be equally significant changes in the composition of that population. Future high school graduates will come from increasingly diverse backgrounds and arguably present additional challenges as well as new opportunities for all of higher education. Demographers indicate "the pool of high school graduates is projected to become less white, more Hispanic and Asian/Pacific Islander and increasingly located in the South over the coming years."[3]

Reinforcing this picture is the news in recent years of rapid reductions in the high school dropout rate of Hispanic students. According to the Pew Research Center, census data show the high school dropout rate among Hispanics in the USA has fallen substantially to a new low, extending a decades-long decline. The Pew report describes this dramatic turnaround:

> The decline in the Hispanic dropout rate is particularly noteworthy given the large increase in Hispanic enrollment in U.S. public and private schools. Between 1999 and 2016, the number of Hispanics enrolled in public and private nursery schools, K-12 schools and colleges increased 80%, from 9.9 million to 17.9 million. By comparison, enrollment during the same period increased 30% among Asians (from 3.6 million to 4.7 million) and 4% among blacks (from 11.3 million to 11.7 million) while falling 14% among whites (from 47.3 million to 40.6 million). Total public school enrollment grew 7%, from 72.4 million to 77.2 million.[4]

This reduction in the Hispanic high school dropout rate has been followed by a long-term increase in Hispanic college enrollment, which is at a record high. The Pew report describes this equally important dynamic:

> A record 3.6 million Hispanics were enrolled in public and private colleges in the U.S. in 2016, up 180% from the 1.3 million who were enrolled in 1999. The increase in Hispanic college enrollment outpaced Hispanic enrollment growth in U.S. nursery and K-12 schools during the same span.[5]

The implications of these changes in the number and composition of the college-age population for colleges and universities may be substantial: It will require greater and more effective emphases on recruiting minority students, first-generation students and, equally important, developing effective strategies that will improve retention of these more financially vulnerable students. Colleges and universities will need to develop successful strategies for closing the long-standing gap in retention and graduation rates that currently exist between the shrinking traditional students and the new generations of minority students moving through the K-12 system.

These projections also indicate significant regional and even state-by-state differences in the number of high school graduates that constitute the student market for our colleges and universities. The Northeast and Midwest are in line to witness the greatest declines in high school graduates with the West likely to see slight increases. The winner among regions will be the South which will likely see "steady, significant increases."

There is little evidence that our nation's institutions of higher education are fully prepared for demographic changes that are in the works. Cogent admissions officers with their student recruitment staffs will need to begin thinking and acting more strategically with a stronger focus on best practices and "what works" in recruiting minority, low income, and other non-traditional students. However, successful recruitment is only half of the challenge; the second and perhaps more difficult challenge is developing campus strategies to successfully retain these new, first-generation minority and non-traditional students through to graduation.

In the decade ahead, institutional enrollment will need to become an even higher priority issue on the agendas of university leaders and their boards. Demographically, this will be a very dynamic and challenging period that may require significant adjustments in college and university policies, institutional budgets, and procedures and practices to meet the changing needs of future cohorts of students. The major concern is whether institutions will be able and willing to make the necessary changes in their recruitment processes and procedures as well as their retention strategies in time to capture and retain student bodies of sufficient size to sustain quality standards or even remain economically viable.

One of the more persistent challenges facing higher education is the continuing uneven graduation rates of students from different ethnic populations. Despite all the research and even modest progress in recent years, the differences in rates of graduation continue to be quite pronounced and socially and economically significant. The persistence of these important differences begs the question: What must colleges and universities do, perhaps differently, to reduce and eliminate these racial and ethnic differences in completion and graduation rates?

Illustrative of these differences are the comparisons reported by the National Student Clearinghouse in "Completing College: A National View of Student Attainment by Race and Ethnicity—Fall 2010 Cohort." Study findings show, for example, that nationally, 62.4% of students in the 2010 cohort completed a degree or certificate in six years. Over two-thirds of white students (67.2%) and more than seven-in-ten Asian students (71.7%) completed a degree within the same six-year period. The completion rates for Hispanics and black population, however, were well below the national level (55.0 and 45.9%, respectively).[6]

Just over half (54.8%) of all students who started any type of college or university in Fall 2010 completed their studies with a degree or certificate in six years. However, when these findings are examined by race and ethnicity, Asian and white students had much higher completion rates (63.2 and 62.0%, respectively) than Hispanic and black students (45.8 and 38.0%, respectively). These rates account for full- and part-time students as well as those who graduated after a transfer. These same racial and ethnic patterns are also found among students who enrolled in community colleges.[7]

Nearly every college and university in the nation has embraced the value and importance of recruiting and admitting racially and ethnically diverse students. Not only is this good admissions policy, it is good education policy, i.e., learning with and about people from different backgrounds and experiences. However, when measured in terms of outcomes, the nation's institutions of higher education are failing to achieve even roughly similar graduation rates. One might be willing to give colleges and universities a "pass" if the racial and ethnic differences were small or modest; however, these differences continue to be large and significant to a degree that falls short of any reasonable definition of a "pass."

These problematic challenges are not evenly distributed among institutions. For example, a recent study of top-tier universities actually found the share of students who are black has actually dropped since 1994. Indiana University's Center for Postsecondary Research found that among the 100 "very high research activity" universities, most "saw their percentage of black undergraduates shrink between 1994 and 2013."[8]

This is clearly one of the demographic challenges facing higher education, i.e., producing completion outcomes where racial and ethnic differences are insignificant or, better, nonexistent. We know from decades of research and experience that college completion brings important benefits not only to the individuals graduating but also to their communities and society in general. These benefits include employment, job satisfaction, civic engagement, personal health as well as economic growth and international competitiveness in the global marketplace.[9]

The question is, how long are we willing to tolerate these differences... these *outcomes*...and still consider our missions fulfilled by faculty and administrators, boards of trustees, accrediting bodies or the taxpayers who subsidize public higher education? For more than a half century, colleges and universities have proclaimed strategic goals and objectives aimed at eliminating these inequalities. It is unfortunate in the extreme that these goals have not been realized largely due to the lack of effective strategies, a sense of urgency and leadership. These inequalities in postsecondary college completion rates "highlight the need for higher education stakeholders to design initiatives aimed at increasing participation and ameliorating racial disparities."[10]

Demographic challenges facing higher education manifest themselves in other important ways, e.g., diversity among faculty, gender differences, and international students. It is ironic, given the expressed value orientation of most universities combined with the years of research and documentation of these problems carried out by faculty, that universities continue to report unexplained, unaddressed racial, ethnic, and gender differences among students, faculty, staff, and administrations.

There are few places where the interaction of demographic and economic factors is greater or takes on more significance than among university students, their families, and college-related decisions. We know, for example, that students from families with high incomes receive more financial assistance from their families for college than students from low-income families. Students from low-income families tend to seek college loans in greater amounts than students from higher-income families. It is also true that the attrition rates of students differ by family income: Students from low-income families drop out at higher rates than those from upper-income families.

One of the unfortunate realities of the current pricing of and financial aid for higher education is the disproportionate economic impact it has on students dropping out of college. Low-income students who borrow significant sums to attend college and for whatever reason leave college often do so with student loans that they find very difficult or impossible to repay. Almost a third of American students who take out loans to pay for college don't get a degree.

Adult and Other Non-traditional Students

One of the most important demographics impacting universities is the growing number of adult students or, in the language of universities, non-traditional students. Observers of university demographics are now telling us that today's non-traditional student is becoming the "new traditional" student. Their numbers are growing at a rate that is making non-traditional students the largest student population on many campuses.

Growth in the non-traditional student population has given rise to increased discussion and research. Who are these non-traditional students and why are their numbers increasing nationally? The National Center for Education Statistics defines this subgroup of students largely in terms of age (25 and over) but also describes age as a "surrogate variable" that "captures a large, heterogeneous population of adult students who often have family and work responsibilities as well as other life circumstances that can interfere with successful completion of educational objectives." The Center also identifies characteristics that are frequently used to describe non-traditional students including race and gender, off-campus residence, employment—particularly those who are working full time, and also enrolled in non-degree occupational programs.[11]

The growing numbers of non-traditional students across the country foretell a quiet demographic revolution underway in American higher education that is reshaping not only the way we pursue a college degree but, increasingly, the way we perceive the university experience. The continuing escalation in tuition, mandatory fees, room, board, books, and associated costs are forcing ever larger numbers of students to find affordable alternative ways of pursuing their education goals. This alternative, non-traditional approach leads them to a very different educational experience including enrolling in early morning classes before they begin their workday, evening classes, weekend courses, independent study, condensed summer programs, and more online courses. For most non-traditional students, their course of study is a patchwork of classes that fits their schedules which, over several years or decades, allows them to meet the requirements for a degree and graduation.

The quiet but steady growth in the non-traditional student population has created a backlog of unmet needs long overlooked by many universities. Office hours for university services, childcare, availability of faculty, and all the services and conveniences typically available to traditional, full time, residential day students become difficult or impossible for non-traditional students to fit into their schedules. In addition to being older, non-traditional students often have other characteristics and challenges that set them apart from their traditional peers. A larger proportion are married or divorced; many are parents including some who are single parents; most are active in the workforce and have full- or part-time jobs; health status and health-care needs may differ; distance to the campus and travel time are factors affecting their schedules and budgets; and most have very limited or no time for campus activities, events, or social life.

College and university policies, programs, and services are generally geared to the needs of traditional, on-campus students. These campus amenities and services, geared to the needs and schedules of traditional students, are often biased against or ignorant of the needs of adult learners and frequently become obstacles to non-traditional students. Consequently, in addition to situational, dispositional, and academic barriers, non-traditional students experience *institutional* barriers to their education not experienced by traditional students. Among the institutional barriers most frequently identified include difficulty in obtaining financial aid, negative attitudes toward older learners, a general lack of resources at times and places convenient to adult students and lack of recognition of academic credentials and prior learning.[12]

Failure to recognize and to adequately address the educational needs of the growing population of adult and non-traditional students represents one of the more important deficiencies in American higher education. For many institutions of higher learning, this failure may be more by design than ignorance, resulting from a preference for the traditional student. This preference may be driven as much by cost considerations associated with providing amenities and services for non-traditional students as by mission, image, reputation, and branding of the college or university.

Many traditional colleges and universities serving traditional students have long overlooked and are institutionally ignorant of the special characteristics and needs of adult and non-traditional students. Even more concerning is the fact that adult and non-traditional students are largely invisible to higher education, especially first-tier universities.[13] An American Council for Education (ACE) survey found that over 40% of institutions indicated that they "did not identify older adult students for purposes of outreach, programs and services, or financial aid." When they do, the prevailing view of adult learners is that they are "one-dimensional" focused predominantly on lifelong learning.[14]

The substantial barriers faced by non-traditional students—personal, situational, financial, institutional, and others—are rarely understood by or addressed by most traditional institutions. The rigidity of the traditional university culture and aversion to change or adaptation is reflected in their negative or lack of response to this important, growing student market.

The uncertain future of American higher education is in many ways linked to the ways our colleges and universities choose to meet the needs and demands for postsecondary and higher learning. In the case of adult and non-traditional students, observers of academe and education policy analysts believe our institutions "don't go far enough" to meet their needs for learning and certification.[15] Others argue that the "traditional path to earning a degree takes too long for students in the workforce" and that the "educational process needs to be reorganized to fit the reality of the needs of working adults."[16]

The Lumina Foundation has been among the nation's leading organizations calling attention to and designing programs to address this major gap and unmet need in American higher education. According to the Foundation, nearly one of every six US residents between the ages of 25 and 64 has some education beyond high school but has not yet earned a degree. Many other adults have not yet started toward an initial credential such as certification, or associate degree. Jamie Merisotis, president and CEO of the Lumina Foundation, urges colleges and universities to "think about how you are delivering education to all the students you are serving…Don't assume that serving [adult] students is an add-on—that is, it has to be part of the fundamental change that I think most institutions are now exploring."[17]

The impetus for change, unfortunately, is *not* coming from colleges and universities but from foundations such as the Lumina Foundation and other organizations. Even more problematic for non-traditional students is the fact that certain traditional higher education systems, policies, and structures are barriers to entry and obstacles to academic progress, certification, and even graduation.[18]

Overlooking the needs and opportunities inherent in the non-traditional student population, ironically, works against the interests of colleges and universities as they encounter increased competition for students. The National Center for Education Statistics estimates that for the foreseeable future the adult learner market is projected to grow at a rate faster than the traditional, late adolescent student market. It would be in their institutional interest for colleges and universities to recognize and adapt to the special circumstances and needs of this important adult, non-traditional student population.

International Student Population

American universities have been attracting international students for over a hundred and fifty years. There has always been a quality in American higher education that has attracted world attention and the interest of bright students from scores of nations. That quality continues to inspire students from around the world who seek to study and learn at the world's finest universities.

I've had the special opportunity to meet young people throughout Asia, the Middle East, and Europe who dream of coming to study at an American university…particularly one that is well known and highly ranked. I've spoken to audiences of students in multiple countries that aspire to attend an American university; I've also addressed audiences of parents whose dreams were to send their child to an American college or university. However, the luster of American colleges and universities, undimmed for decades, is beginning to be less attractive due to the growing strength of higher education in many other parts of the world as well as changes in the image and brand of American higher education.

Currently, the number of international students enrolling in US colleges and universities continues to grow. In 2016/2017, nearly 35,000 more international students came to American universities bringing the total to 1,078,822, a 3.4% increase over the previous year and an 85% increase over the previous decade. These figures, reported by the Institute of International Education (IIE) in their publication, *Open Doors*, reflect the eleventh consecutive year of expansion in the total number of international students enrolled in US colleges and universities.[19]

IIE also reports that international students constitute just over 5% of the more than 20 million students enrolled in US colleges and universities. This percentage has increased in the last decade due to the growing number of international students and the declines in the number of American students enrolled.

The million-plus international students bring a significant value-added quality to American higher education. In addition to the $39 billion in revenue to US colleges and universities are the non-monetary values of increased cultural diversity, greater understanding of cultural differences, and the international relationships spawned that often endure for lifetimes. The presence of international students on American college and university campuses has enhanced the quality of the educational experience as well as the financial health of the institutions. In a very real sense, the high quality of many American institutions of higher education is due in part to the multicultural, international character of faculties and student bodies.

China continues to send the largest number of student to US colleges and universities. One-third of all international students, 350,755, come from China. India sends the second largest number of students, 186,267, or 17.3%. Together, China and India contribute half of the international students to US colleges and universities. In 2016/2017, South Korea sent 58,663 students, Saudi Arabia sent 52,611, and Canada sent 27,065. It is significant that the number of students from Saudi Arabia decreased by 14.2% from the previous year.

The international student scene, however, is showing signs of change that will, in all probability, impact higher education in the USA, its enrollment, and cultural diversity. International enrollment in the USA began to flatten in 2016, partly because of changing conditions abroad and in the USA. Among the changes is the rapid growth of universities in China and other nations. The BBC reported in 2016 that China was opening a new university every week.[20] Similarly, India plans to have 278 new universities, 388 colleges according to the nation's Higher Education Secretary.[21] Other nations that have been sending large numbers of students to American institutions are currently developing plans of their own that not only include building new universities but upgrading the quality of their existing institutions.

Intergovernmental relations and international politics also play a role in the number of international students coming to the USA to study. Increased uncertainty in US foreign policy, trade policy, and openness to foreign students could substantially alter the size of the international student population. Certainly, America's image in the world and its reputation for welcoming immigrants and foreigners is changing which will, in all likelihood, have an impact on the attractiveness of US colleges and universities to international students.

Many US colleges and universities have benefited significantly—financially, culturally, and educationally—during the past decade by the ever larger numbers of international students. Some American colleges and universities have become financially dependent on the revenue from international student tuition and fees. However, plans and developments underway in China, India, and many other nations to build larger, more robust higher education infrastructures could bring significant reductions in the numbers of international student attending US institutions. The added concern that could make current patterns even more problematic for American colleges and universities is changes in US foreign policy, trade policy, visa policy, and international relations, generally. International student enrollments are sensitive to the international policy environment and perceptions of those policies. What was once a very welcoming country for international students could change quite rapidly bringing significant reductions in this important student population.

The uncertain future of American public universities is made even more uncertain by potential decreases in international student enrollment. Many factors and conditions that influence and even control the flow of international students to US campuses are currently in play. The effects of 9/11 and tighter controls on international student visas by the Department of Homeland Security is just one example. Early signs of potential changes in the number of international students were seen in 2016/2017. The full extent of future changes in international student enrollment in US institutions is not known; however, education policy makers and leaders of universities that currently serve significant numbers of international students should not assume these numbers will grow or even remain constant. Conditions that could bring significant decreases in international student enrollment in American colleges and universities are apparent and apt to bring such change in the near future unless a more welcoming image of the country is promoted by the nation's leadership.

Conclusions: Considerations and Concerns

The forces of demography—growth, composition, distribution, and movement of populations—play a major role in higher education. Higher education leaders and policy makers are generally aware of major, national demographic trends that are known to impact our colleges and universities, e.g., the postwar baby boom and the increasing diversity of the nation's population. But the more subtle, less visible, ongoing changes in national, regional, and local populations are seldom studied for their impact on particular institutions. Natural increases and decreases in populations and resulting changes in the size of cities, states, and regions are seldom studied or perhaps even recognized by higher education policy makers and leaders. Other than occasional media coverage of a "brain drain" in their city or region, changes in migration patterns—both in- and out-migrations—seldom get the recognition their importance deserves from the perspective of their impact on area institutions of higher education. Likewise, changes in the composition of populations in terms of ethnicity and associated socioeconomic characteristics rarely figure into enrollment forecasts for institutions of higher education.

Leaders of the nation's institutions of higher education may feel or assume they are capable of addressing the coming challenges of demographic change. Unfortunately, these population-based challenges—some of which are outlined in this chapter—are only one set of challenges among a host of other serious destabilizing disruptions and concerns. It is the combination of challenges, noted previously, interacting that make the coming decade one that requires extraordinary understanding, effective strategies, efficient operations, and strong leadership.

Demographic changes—domestic and international—must figure prominently in the strategic planning for our colleges, universities, and higher education, generally. This is not only the responsibility of university leaders and their boards of trustees; it is the responsibility of governors and legislators to ensure the continued health, vitality, efficacy, and relevance of their public colleges and universities. Governors are in a particularly strategic position to help influence national policies impacting the attractiveness of American colleges and universities to international students. Individual governors and the National Governors Association should be major players in shaping the image and policies that continue to make USA attractive and welcoming to international students.

References

1. WICHE, *Knocking at the College Door, Projections of High School Graduates, 2016* (December 20, 2017).
2. Ibid.
3. Rick Seltzer, "The High School Graduate Plateau," *Inside Higher Ed* (December 6, 2016).
4. John Gramlich, *Hispanic Dropout Rate Hits New Low, College Enrollment at New High* (Pew Research Center, September 29, 2017).
5. Ibid.
6. D. Shapiro, A. Dunbar, F. Huie, P. Wakhungu, X. Yuan, A. Nathan, and Y. Hwang, *A National View of Student Attainment Rates by Race and Ethnicity—Fall 2010 Cohort* (Herndon, VA: National Student Clearinghouse Research Center, 2017).
7. Ibid.
8. Indiana University Center for Postsecondary Research cited in, Andrew McGill, "The Missing Black Students at Elite American Universities," *The Atlantic* (November 23, 2015).
9. L. DeAngelo, R. Franke, S. Hurtado, J. H. Pryor, and S. Tran, *Completing College: Assessing Graduation Rates at Four-Year Institutions* (UCLA: Higher Education Research Institute, 2011).
10. D. Shapiro, A. Dunbar, F. Huie, P. Wakhungu, X. Yuan, A. Nathan, and Y. Hwang, ibid.
11. National Center for Education Statistics, "Who Is Nontraditional?," *Definitions and Data* (U.S. Department of Education, no date).
12. Dorthy MacKeracher, Theresa Suart, and Judith Potter, *State of the Field Report: Barriers to Participation in Adult Learning* (Fredericton, New Brunswick: National Adult Literacy Database, 2006).
13. X. Coulter and X. Mandell, "Adult Higher Education: Are We Moving in the Wrong Direction?," *Journal of Continuing Higher Education* (Volume 60), 40–42, cited in Joseph C. Chen, "Nontraditional Adult Learners:

The Neglected Diversity in Postsecondary Education," *Sage Open* (January–March 2017), 1–12.
14. Joseph C. Chen, ibid.
15. Stephen G. Pelletier, *Success for Adult Students* (Public Purpose, Fall, 2010).
16. Brian Bosworth, cited in Stephen G. Pelletier, ibid.
17. Jamie Merisotis, cited in Stephen G. Pelletier, ibid.
18. Ty M. Cruce and Nicholas W. Hillman, "Preparing for the Silver Tsunami: The Demand for Higher Education Among Older Adults," *Research in Higher Education* (Volume 53, 2012) 593–613.
19. "2017 Open Doors Report on International Educational Exchange," *Institute of International Education* (November 13, 2017).
20. Andreas Schleicher, "China Opens a New University Every Week," *BBC News* (March 16, 2016).
21. "India to Have 278 New Universities, 388 Colleges: Higher Education Secretary," *DECCAN Chronicle* (November 25, 2013).

11

University Governance: Structures, Roles, and Responsibilities

The relevance, quality, and sustainability of our public colleges and universities are ultimately functions of enlightened and effective governance. Interestingly, at least in the USA, university governance is viewed very narrowly and operationally. When the topic of university governance surfaces—which it rarely does—it is most often referring to boards of trustees, i.e., the "governing body" of the university. While university governing boards are an important component of university governance, the notion or concept of governance as it relates to public higher education in the USA is much broader, more complex, and in need of attention.

The unsettling challenges facing public higher education in the USA have become so pronounced that serious efforts to address these issues must include an assessment of the role, capacity, and effectiveness of higher education governing bodies and processes. Traditional approaches, structures, and policies in place to provide accountability and quality assurance, oversight and leadership for our institutions increasingly fall short of the growing demands for a system of governance that serves the broader needs and interests of higher education.[1]

These changing conditions beg the questions: Are the structures, systems, and bodies that provide governance, oversight, and accountability for our public colleges and universities sufficient and capable of governing our institutions of higher education effectively in this era of escalating costs, disruptive technologies, and changing demographics? Are the problems facing public higher education solvable within the framework, structures, norms, and practices of their governing bodies? Are there different approaches or improvements to the structures and systems that would better serve the governing needs, challenges, and opportunities facing public higher education?

The sustainability of public higher education systems or important parts of these systems that meet the changing needs of American society is being called into question. It is increasingly important, perhaps essential, for those charged with leading, governing, and providing oversight of public higher education engage in constructive introspection and meaningful self-assessment to ensure that governance structures, processes, and practices are in place, operating effectively and are successfully addressing the challenges. Without capable, effective governance, public higher education will lack the oversight, guidance, and policies it needs to remain sustainable and to meet the looming challenges and uncertainties ahead.

Responsibilities of Governing Networks and Bodies

The governance structures of public universities are state-based and operate within the constitutions, statutes, policies, and regulations of their respective states. There is also considerable variation among the states in the nature, size, number, organization, and performance of higher education governance structures. Over the past century, state university governance structures have grown and developed into one of several models. These models range from states where universities are autonomous and operate independently under state legislatures to models that have a designated organization to coordinate or control the institutions. In effect, there are "non-systems," state "systems" of higher education and, in a few of the larger states there are multiple systems or a "system of systems."

In a very real sense, the quality and effectiveness of our universities depend on the quality and effectiveness of governance. Governance structures provide the philosophical, political, and fiduciary environment within which universities function and respond to the ever-evolving, rapidly changing needs of the workforce and society. Within these environments, colleges, and universities have, for the past two decades, been under growing pressures from legislatures and accrediting bodies to become more "accountable." Accrediting bodies are demanding that more attention be given to "outcomes" and are requiring measures of these outcomes through campus-wide assessments. Governing bodies of state institutions and systems, however, have little or no such pressures and tend to function, with varying degrees of accountability, under the broad, often distant, oversight of state legislatures and governors.

Viability and sustainability of our nation's public colleges and universities as well as our leadership among nations with respect to higher education is not solely the responsibility of individual institutions and their institutional governing boards. The common practice of viewing the quality, viability, and sustainability of our public colleges and universities as the sole responsibility of their respective governing boards of trustees, regents, or visitors is wildly misplaced. Governing public higher education in the states is the responsibility of a broader network of players. This network starts with governors but also includes legislatures, departments of education and higher education, coordinating boards, controlling boards, regents, secretaries/chancellors overseeing higher education as well as university governing boards. A new more holistic perspective that recognizes the importance of all the various parties in the governing network and their roles in governance is long past due.

Holistic Governance

Governance of our public colleges and universities has many players with each playing their unique and obligatory roles. These players perform roles and engage in defined relationships that vary somewhat from state to state but in the final analysis, every public college or university operates within an accountability structure that works on behalf of the citizens and taxpayers who help fund public higher education. The key players in the governance network and structures, noted above, perform important roles, engage in relationships, and make policy and funding decisions that enable the institutions to achieve their missions and play their role in the states' systems of higher education.

The challenges facing higher education increasingly demand a more cohesive, integrated, holistic approach to governance. Greater clarity is also needed regarding the roles of the several players in the governance system, e.g., the governor, legislature, and others in the governance network. What is the role and responsibility of governors for the proper, effective governance and oversight of their state's colleges and universities and, do we hold them accountable in any formal sense—constitutional or statutory—other than through elections? The same questions need to be asked about state legislatures: How do we hold them accountable other than through elections?

These may be among the more important questions with respect to the quality and performance of our public colleges and universities but are almost never asked by accrediting bodies or even the public through any formal process. The future of public higher education—its viability, quality, and sustainability—will require a more holistic approach to governance where *all* the relevant players are held accountable. A more holistic approach to governance needs to replace the piecemeal system that now places most, if not all, the responsibility for the viability and sustainability of our colleges and universities on individual boards of trustees, regents, and visitors with no accountability expected from the most powerful and influential state officials. Holistic governance more clearly identifies *all* policy-making parties that play a role in insuring the states' postsecondary and higher education needs are met and the institutions remain viable and sustainable. This is a major responsibility of statewide elected officials.

Strong Governance Begins with State Constitutions

State constitutions address issues determined to exceed in importance those issues normally addressed by statute. In contemporary knowledge-based economies, the critical importance of higher education to states, their economies, workforces, and citizens meets the standard for inclusion in state constitutions. Good governance of higher education requires recognition by states and their legislative bodies of this importance and taking steps to ensure appropriate constitutional provisions are made to ensure quality and sustainability in their public colleges and universities.

There are some similarities but also many differences among state constitutions. State constitutions differ in length and have different origins and perform somewhat different functions. Over time, states have adopted constitutional provisions covering a wide range of issues usually reflecting the major concerns of the state at the time of their adoption.

One of the most important roles of states—establishing, maintaining, and supporting tertiary, postsecondary education—gets scant attention in many state constitutions. Most states describe and define their obligations and responsibilities for higher education through statutes while constitutional provisions, where they do exist, articulate the autonomy of public colleges and universities and, in some instances, state the limits of governmental interference in institutional operations.[2]

The role and provisions of state constitutions as the foundation for sound governance and the sustainability of public higher education has become increasingly important in recent decades as competing interests for state support have grown. Health care, prisons, transportation, and other interests have increased the pressures on legislative bodies and governors to shift funds needed to ensure quality higher education to these other areas. Constitutional protections of public higher education, one of the states' most important responsibilities, are now needed in every state to enable their colleges and universities to meet the growing demands for an educated workforce and the needs of the states' economies.

Constitutional grounding and protections have become increasingly important in recent years as state funding for public colleges and universities has declined and become more problematic. Recognizing this importance, State Higher Education Executive Officers (SHEEO) requested information from state Finance Officers about their state's constitution and any provisions for financial support of their states' colleges and universities. In this 2014 inquiry, they asked: *"Does your state constitution include provisions that describe sufficiency of funding to maintain a system of public institutions of higher education? If so, what are they?"*[3]

Of the twenty-seven states responding to the inquiry, only five indicated any form of constitutional support for higher education: Arizona, Nevada, North Carolina, North Dakota, and Wyoming. Even among these five states, there is considerable variation in their level of commitment to "sufficiency of funding." Only two states appear to make a firm constitutional provision for ensuring their institutions have sufficient funding.[4]

One can only speculate about the reasons for this lack of constitutional protections of higher education. It may be that constitutions were adopted at earlier times when K-12 was the most important education issue. It could also be that no organized efforts to adopt constitutional status and protections have been made. Presumably, it could also be a calculated strategy by state leaders and legislators to avoid constitutional responsibilities associated with maintaining a strong system of higher education so they can continue to shift the burden of ever-larger portions of the cost to students and their families.

Strong systems of public higher education require the commitment and support of their respective states. The strongest commitment a state can make to their public colleges and universities and their sustainability is to enshrine that support through constitutional provisions. Every state has a deeply embedded vested interest in strong, high-quality institutions of higher education. This interest will only grow stronger in the future. The economy of every state is dependent on the stream of college and university graduates to fill needed positions in the professions and workforce. Every metropolitan region and community—rural and urban—is dependent on the knowledge and expertise nurtured and conveyed by their state colleges and universities. Every state is equally dependent on the innovations, research, health care, expertise, and leadership produced by their institutions of higher education.

Perhaps it goes without saying, strong, sustainable public colleges and universities also require good, effective, and responsible governance. Good governance of higher education starts with a firm commitment in unequivocal language in the states' constitutions. Those states that enshrine their commitment to higher education in their constitutions provide a stronger foundation for their colleges and universities and strengthen their sustainability and leadership in the challenging years ahead.

State Structures of Higher Education

Among the concepts of public college and university governance is the legal principle of "constitutional autonomy." This principle makes a state university a "separate department of government, not merely an agency of the executive or legislative branch." States differ, however, in the degree of constitutional autonomy. In his review of constitutional provisions for higher education, N. H. Hutchens offers the following six distinctions that, in effect, form a typology of the degree of institutional autonomy[5]:

I. Substantial Recognition, Extensive Constitutional Autonomy
II. Moderate-Limited Recognition, Degrees of Constitutional Autonomy
III. Judicial Recognition, Constitutional Autonomy Subject to Extensive Legislative Control
IV. Judicial Rejection of Constitutional Autonomy
V. Ambiguous Recognition
VI. No Judicial Recognition/Recognition Doubtful.

Public colleges and universities, operating within these varying degrees of institutional autonomy, are generally governed in one of three ways: (1) consolidated governing board, (2) coordinating board, or (3) planning agency that is either statutory or constitutional.[6]

Consolidated governing boards have "complete authority" over a state's system of public higher education for finances, degrees, personnel, and property. Nine states have one such governing board that oversees all public colleges and universities; fourteen states have separate boards for two-year and four-year institutions. Coordinating boards, unlike governing boards, work with college and university boards "to advance state interests and agendas" without actually controlling the actions of local boards. They promote state priorities, facilitate the transfer of credit, and seek to reduce program duplication among institutions. Some have controls on institutional budgeting. State planning agencies—constitutional and statutory—facilitate coordination among a state's institutions of higher education. This model was more common in the past; only three states currently use the planning mode.

Within this mix of state structures of higher education is the compelling, universal need for colleges and universities to advance the quality of learning and competency required to meet the rapidly growing demands of our knowledge-based and technology-driven society. In their efforts to meet these demands, colleges and universities have been forced to develop new programs, adopt new technologies, enter into new partnerships, and, in the process, have become much more complex organizations. This growing complexity places new demands on governance, demands that have been largely ignored or not even recognized.

There are also the critically important prerequisites of preserving the appropriate levels of autonomy of colleges and universities and the academic freedom of their faculties while maintaining reasonable accountability to the state and its taxpayers supporting the institutions. It can be a difficult balancing act that requires informed leadership and policy at all levels of the governing structure and a commitment to the values that undergird our institutions of higher education. This is the role of good, effective, and responsible governance, i.e., holistic governance.

The Role of Governors

The complexity of issues involved in designing "good governance" should not be underestimated. The politics—partisan and nonpartisan—and strong vested interests surrounding higher education create tensions and conflicts that are not easy to live with nor easily resolved. At the center of this complex, mix of interests and issues is the role played by governors. Some governors run on a platform of becoming an "education governor" and focus their time, energy, and influence on improving K-12 and, occasionally, higher education. There are others who also claim to be "education governors" who, intentionally or unintentionally, have done more damage than good to their state's public education systems and institutions.

The complexities that characterize higher education governance create opportunities as well as challenges for governors. These have been described in a valuable case study by Robert Berdahl in "Strong Governors and Higher Education: A Survey and Analysis." While the focus of Berdahl's case study is the State of Maryland, the lessons learned, particularly about the intricacies and implications of board and other appointments, can be applied in other states.

The power of governors to influence the quality and sustainability of public higher education is probably unsurpassed by any person in the state. Perhaps it goes without saying that the power held by governors should *not* be used for partisan ends but rather to ensure strong, effective governance of colleges and universities. Many governors have viewed their roles in university governance as simply making appointments to university boards and weighing in on budget matters that relate to state subsidies for higher education. Others have demonstrated a much stronger, more intrusive role by manipulating established processes and using executive decisions and appointments which, in some instances, have not been for the purpose of improving governance or the quality of higher education but for greater control or even partisan or ideological objectives.

It is this fear of "manipulating, intrusive" governors or state governments that has so strongly reinforced higher education's insistence on autonomy and freedom from state control. In his study of Maryland's university-government relationship, Robert Berdahl refers to Terry Sanford, former Governor of North Carolina, former President of Duke University, and US Senator from that state. Sanford in his book, *Storm over the States* (1967), worried that independent boards were in danger of being "captured" by professionals in higher education and that "these professionals did not always have the broader public interest in mind when making policy."[7] It was Sanford's view that

...the Governor was usually in a better position to define and protect the public interest and noted that "more universities have suffered from political indifference than have ever been upset by political interference." In his view a Governor who had more political influence with the independent boards would be more likely to throw financial and policy support to their recommendations.[8]

A different, more recent perspective emerges from many in Ohio's higher education community in response to Governor Kasich's changes in the way higher education is represented in state government. Great concern is being expressed over the inability of the Ohio Board of Regents to meet for over a year because it has only two members of a nine-member board and lacks three to constitute a quorum required for meetings. Governor Kasich made no appointments to the Ohio Board of Regents for a five year period. Even greater concern is coming from the higher education community in response to the governor's support for a bill that combines the state's K-12 school, university, and workforce development systems into a single new Department of Learning and Achievement.[9]

Central to the role of governors in relation to higher education are listening and regular communication with university presidents and their boards. All parties—governors, presidents, and boards of trustees or regents—benefit from exchanging views and learning from other key higher education leaders. Annual retreats, hosted by governors for presidents and boards, in addition to other ways of communicating, will benefit colleges and universities that make up state systems. Governors should make periodic visits to campuses to meet with students, faculty, and administrators to hear their concerns and to provide a forum for policy discussions with those charged with implementing policies at the institution level.

The opportunities for governors to have a positive impact on their state's public colleges and universities as well as private institutions are substantial. As one of the states' largest expenditures, higher education clearly justifies a portion of the governors' time and attention. Governors can make the difference between strong, positive governance and governance that fails to meet the needs and demands of public higher education.

Trustees and Regents in Shared Governance

Much has been written about college and university governing boards and their key role in establishing and maintaining the quality, strength, reputations, and sustainability of their institutions. Entire organizations and associations have been formed to help support governing boards in the performance of their critically important role. Numerous conferences, workshops, and webinars are held annually to provide instruction and guidance to governing board members, trustees, and regents. Likewise, numerous consulting firms have sprouted over the past few decades to help boards when they find themselves in difficulty or seem unable to solve their problems without assistance. An entire industry has grown into maturity in recent years geared to helping college and university boards with the never-ending stream of challenges that confront our institutions of higher education.

Public colleges and universities are highly complex organizations that must be responsive to multiple constituents including, among others, students, parents, donors, alumni, governments (local, state, and federal), public officials, numerous accrediting bodies, businesses and industries, suppliers, athletic booster groups, and taxpayers. The policy-making bodies for public institutions of higher education—those with broad oversight authority—must bring knowledge, experience, and some degree of sophistication to their decision-making processes if institutions are to fulfill their missions, meet the needs of the states they serve and develop their full potential.

Many members of public college and university governing boards fall short of this minimum standard. Governing board members in most states—with only four exceptions—are appointed by governors. James J. Duderstadt, former president of the University of Michigan, addresses this issue head-on in his work, *A University for the 21st Century* (2000): "The process of gubernatorial appointment" he argues, "is not yielding the quality of trustees necessary to govern the contemporary university."[10]

Unfortunately, the expertise needs of boards are seldom the criteria for selecting new members; it is rare when governors even know the needs of the boards for which they are selecting members. With few exceptions, new university board members selected by governors are members of the governor's political party, often donors to their campaigns, or a relative or friend of someone important who needs to be rewarded. These valued appointments bring prestige and perks that many find enticing including invitations to the president's loge for sports events, public recognition by the president, invitations to performing arts events, and more. They also bring a significant opportunity for public service and civic engagement.

Duderstadt takes aim at the governing board appointment practices and, quite correctly, argues that the complexities of modern universities require governing boards of "great experience and distinction...To allow political patronage or party politics to determine board membership is to court disaster."[11] The selection of trustees needs greater attention and reforms to meet the increasing challenges and complexities of contemporary colleges and universities. Duderstadt and others argue that, in most instances, trustee appointments are falling short of what is required by our institutions' governing boards.

Governing boards establish various committees to review, discuss, and offer proposals and motions for board action. These committees usually include committees on academic affairs, student affairs, budget and fiscal affairs, facilities, legal affairs, and a variety of other administrative domains. Many create an executive committee to work closely with the president and administration when needed. Executive committees usually consist of the chairs of the other board committees and play an active role in the board oversight function.

It would be difficult to assign priorities to board functions: they are responsible for broad oversight of the institution and all that entails. However, institutional finances will be at the top or near the top of every member's concerns. Donald Kennedy expresses this view in unambiguous language: "Permanence and fidelity are more than the devout wishes of founders and legislators. They are binding legal requirements on trustees, that is, matters of *fiduciary duty*...this encourages, indeed compels, a certain level of devotion."[12]

The fiduciary responsibility of governing boards is not limited to the immediate needs, challenges, and opportunities that occupy most of their time; rather, fiduciary responsibility extends well into the future with obligatory consideration to the strength of their university for future students, faculty, administrators, and boards. Every decision and action taken by governing boards should be preceded by a discussion or clear understanding of the long-term impact of the decision on students and the institution in addition to the immediate impact being sought by the decision-makers.

Unlike corporate boards, college and university boards of trustees work with faculty—usually through representatives of faculty organizations such as faculty senates—and the administration through what has become known as "shared governance." The concept of shared governance gained broad support in the 1960s when several higher education associations together with AAUP issued statements in support of governing boards sharing governing activities and responsibilities with faculty, particularly in academic policy making.

The problem with shared governance is that so few faculties or trustees who adhere to it as the model for college or university governance truly understand what it means. A 2009 article in the Chronicle of Higher Education emphasized this point:

> The phrase shared governance is so hackneyed that it is becoming what some linguists call an "empty" or "floating" signifier, a term so devoid of determinate meaning that it takes on whatever significance a particular speaker gives it at the moment. Once a term arrives at that point, it is essentially useless.[13]

The more serious problem with the notion of shared governance is that no matter how a particular board chooses to *share* their governance activities, there is no actual sharing of governance responsibility. Governing boards are the responsible entity with respect to the oversight of *all* college and university functions, domains, policies, and programs. Delegating some activities to the president or faculty or any person or group does not absolve the governing board of any governing duties and responsibilities. Even in a shared governance arrangement common on most college and university campuses, there is no formal sharing of authority or responsibility.

The value in shared governance is not the formal responsibility or accountability for policies or actions of the institution; rather, it is the collegial drive to gain informed participation in decision-making. As Olson pointed out in the Chronicle of Higher Education, "genuine shared governance gives voice (but not necessarily ultimate authority) to concerns common to all constituencies as well as to issues to specific groups."

University governance is, for the most part, in the hands of appointed laypersons who may or may not have the background, knowledge, or expertise needed to govern these large, complex, very specialized organizations. Governors making these appointments are in a position to significantly improve public college and university governance by insisting or even requiring new board members complete an institution-sponsored workshop or, preferably, an orientation to their new duties and responsibilities provided by the Association of University Governing Boards (AGB) or any number of other organizations or consulting firms with in-depth knowledge of public higher education governance. Experienced board members can also serve as mentors to new members to help bring them up to speed on protocols, policies, programs, and major issues with which the board is dealing. Boards and their members who attend AGB conferences and workshops and invest time in reading their publications and briefings will be better prepared for understanding the background and issues that continually work their way up to the board agenda.

Autonomy and Accountability

The autonomy/accountability question is, perhaps, the major issue in the governance of public colleges and universities. Each concept is important but the continuing conversation centers on the amount of autonomy needed for universities to function appropriately in a free and open democracy. The second part of the issue centers on the need for public universities to be fully accountable to the state and, ultimately, the taxpayers that fund public higher education.

The autonomy/accountability calculus is, in many respects, the "freedom/responsibility" question. Just as there is no freedom without responsibility, there can be no autonomy without accountability. The question is how can public colleges and universities and the states that fund them arrive at the proper balance of these two important, sometimes conflicting goals?

Derek Bok and others continue to remind us of the importance of this question: How can we best reconcile the legitimate concerns of government with the essential freedoms of a university? What are these "legitimate concerns" and what are "essential freedoms?" The problems for Bok and policy makers today are in the deciding where to draw the line. "How much autonomy should universities have in carrying out their academic functions?" How can governments and the institutions of higher education work together and each fulfil their respective responsibilities?

Again, Bok provides wise instruction and guidance on this important question: "…public officials need to consider the role of state and university in a larger perspective instead of continuing to act in a piecemeal fashion intervening here and withdrawing there in reaction to a disconnected series of specific problems and special concerns."[14] This challenge of a "larger perspective" is needed and represents a great opportunity for governments and institutions of higher education to chart a course in their relationship that recognizes the interests and responsibilities of both.

Finding the right "balance" and knowing where to "draw the line" between the university need for autonomy and the need of government for accountability is a complex and often stressful process. It requires informed dialogue between and among committed participants. It is, however, incumbent on leaders of both institutions—government and higher education—to pursue this process in creative and imaginative ways, keeping in mind the legitimate needs of both.

Governors, public policy makers, and university leaders, working together, can set the tone for this effort. Governors should be the first to defend the interests of their states' universities need for autonomy while college and university leaders defend government's legitimate expectation for accountability. Again, Bok's wise council is for government to choose "the least intrusive method to achieve its legitimate ends."[15] Likewise, higher education, supported by the state and its taxpayers, should be supportive of non-intrusive accountability for their policies, programs, and actions.

Conclusions and Growing Concerns

There is a growing appreciation for the increasing complexities and challenges facing the nation's public colleges and universities, particularly in view of the shrinking support for public higher education in many states. Public awareness of the increased burden now carried by students and their families for college costs previously covered by states has grown to the point that it is now common knowledge and a national concern. Even more concerning is the view expressed by a growing number of critics that the established governance structures of the nation's institutions of higher education need attention if they are to be able to meet and successfully address these and other growing challenges.

More than a decade ago, Leon Trakman, writing with clear foresight about higher education, expressed these concerns:

> Twentieth century governance models used in public universities are subject to increasing doubt across the English-speaking world. Governments question if public universities are being efficiently governed; if their boards of trustees are adequately fulfilling their trust obligations towards multiple stakeholders; and if collegial models of governance are working in increasingly complex educational environments.[16]

This common concern—phrased diplomatically by most to avoid irresponsible changes or panic—can be found in the writings and speeches of highly respected higher education policy scholars, former presidents, and chancellors of some of our nation's most respected universities and even some of our most conservative higher education associations. This issue has grown to be one of the most pressing concerns in public higher education among those familiar with the actual workings of the current system of college and university governance. The proverbial "can" has been "kicked down the road" for more than a decade with each new year adding indisputable evidence to the argument for reform of the current paradigm and a new, more effective model of university governance.

The new technologies emerging during the past decade alone argue forcefully for rethinking many of our past assumptions and theories about how best to organize and offer higher education as well as the way we pay for and govern our institutions. Concepts of institutional autonomy, shared governance, accountability, state higher education structures, and systems, the role of governors, lay boards, board expertise, and responsibilities, and role of presidents and administrations have not been subject to comprehensive re-examination for a century or ever. These and a myriad of other issues have been left largely unexamined by colleges and universities for so long that it would be difficult to find a state or system that isn't struggling to meet the current challenges, not to mention preparing for the coming major changes that will surely impact higher education and the needs and competencies of learners.

The pragmatist might ask, Who is going to lead this re-examination effort? Who has the trust, moral and legitimate authority, the knowledge and expertise, and political will to call for and lead a re-examination of how we govern our public colleges and universities? These are questions that must soon be answered if we are to salvage the failing infrastructure of our nation's public colleges and universities and meet the challenges of governing our institutions now looming on the horizon.

How is higher education in the twenty-first century to be governed? What are the lessons learned from the twentieth century we can bring to this discussion? What demands will the mid-twenty-first century bring that require advanced learning and organizations/institutions to provide that learning? Who will provide that learning organization? What are the projected costs of these future institutions and how will these costs be covered? How can states better prepare for and make the major changes needed going forward? This is the challenge, indeed, the responsibility of those individuals and officials that are part of the governance structure and network for our colleges and universities.

References and Notes

1. See *State of Our States: What Will Be the Lasting Effects on Higher Education* (Andrew Hibel, HigherEdJobs, no date).
2. Midwest Higher Education Compact, *State Constitutional Provisions and Higher Education Governance: Policy Report* (May 2013).
3. SHEEO Information Request, *Provisions of Funding to Maintain a System of Public Institutions of Higher Education* (December 12, 2014).
4. Ibid.
5. N. H. Hutchens, "Preserving the Independence of Public Higher Education: An Examination of State Constitutional Autonomy Provisions for Public Colleges and Universities," *Journal of College and University Law* (2010), 1–30.
6. Aaron S. Horn, et al., "State Constitutional Provisions and Higher Education Governance: Policy Report," *Midwestern Higher Education Compact* (May 2013).
7. Terry Sanford, *Storm over the States* (New York: McGraw-Hill, 1967).
8. R. O. Berdahl and T. R. McConnell, "Autonomy and Accountability: Who Controls Academe?," in P. G. Altbach, P. J. Gumport, and R. O. Berdahl (eds.), *American Higher Education in the 21st Century* (Baltimore, MD: The Johns Hopkins Press, 2011), 70–88.
9. Karen Farkas, cleveland.com, kfarkas@cleveland.com.
10. James J. Duderstadt, *A University for the 21st Century* (Ann Arbor: University of Michigan Press, 2000), 246.
11. Ibid.
12. Donald Kennedy, *Academic Duty* (Cambridge: Harvard University Press, 1997), 121.
13. Gary A. Olson, "Exactly What Is 'Shared Governance'?," *Chronicle of Higher Education* (July 23, 2009).
14. Derek Bok, *Beyond the Ivory Tower: Social Responsibilities of the Modern University* (Cambridge: Harvard University Press, 1982).
15. Ibid., p. 60.
16. Leon Trakman, "Modeling University Governance," *Higher Education Quarterly* (May 1, 2008).

12

Accreditation: How It Works and Is It Working?

In the late 1990s, I served as a member of an accreditation visiting team to a major Western state university. The university had completed its self-study and was well prepared for the visit. My task was to interview the dean and department chairs in the social and behavioral sciences to ascertain their performance on several accreditation-related standards and issues.

One of those issues was assessment of student outcomes. My request to department chairs was, "Tell me what your department is doing to assess student learning and outcomes." All of the responding department chairs indicated that they "were working on it" or were "just getting underway," or "making progress but have a ways to go." However, one department chair—political science, as I recall—when asked what his department was doing to assess student outcomes, replied: "We are resisting it in every way we can."

This response was followed by the chairman's impassioned commentary and critique of the "corporatization of higher education" and the need for universities to resist and reclaim their autonomy. The chairman's criticism extended to the role regional accrediting bodies were playing in the "corporatization" makeover and how my questions and

© The Author(s) 2019
D. M. Johnson, *The Uncertain Future of American Public Higher Education*,
https://doi.org/10.1007/978-3-030-01794-1_12

those raised by my fellow visiting team members were forcing universities to take responsibility for students' learning, graduation, job placement, and more. From his perspective, the role of the university was to "provide" or make available a quality educational experience; it was the student's responsibility to learn, graduate, and get a job…not his.

In my evaluation and report on his department, the chairman received an "A" for honesty. The substance of this commentary, however, raised questions and some concerns with the visiting accreditation team. I've reflected on the chairman's criticism of the questions we were asking as members of the visitation team and the purpose of these questions: In effect, the chairman was drawing a line of demarkation between those who view the role of universities to "provide and make available" a quality education experience and those who measure college and university quality in terms of student "outcomes," i.e., student learning, graduation rates, employment following graduation, and even career success.

A "line of demarkation" was clearly drawn between those who view the role of accrediting bodies as judging the quality of what is provided—"inputs"—versus what students gained from the education experience—"outcomes." That philosophical difference continues today and, in many ways, points to the ongoing concerns about the purpose and role of accreditation. Are students, their families, and taxpayers getting what they are paying for? Are the citizens, taxpayers, and state getting the needed return on its investment?

This vignette in its own simplistic way—through the honesty of the department chairman—demonstrates at least one of the major issues facing accreditation. But there are many issues and questions surrounding accreditation that, in certain instances, go to the heart of the concerns and controversies about higher education. The conversation—perhaps "debate" is a more accurate description—on accreditation continues. This debate requires resolution, or at least progress toward resolution, if American higher education is to chart a long-term trajectory toward sustainable, affordable, relevant systems, and structures that ensure quality learning experiences for students and meets the needs of society.

What Is Accreditation?

Notwithstanding the national debate, I find it puzzling that accreditation is not well understood, even by those most affected, i.e., university boards of trustees and many university administrators. Few faculty understand it even though they go through the accreditation review process every ten years and more frequently if they are in a professional school or college of business, pharmacy, medicine, etc.

Accrediting agencies describe accreditation as voluntary, non-governmental, self-regulation of higher education that serves two purposes: assuring the public of quality academic programs and fostering institutional improvement. Regional groupings of postsecondary institutions essentially agree to judge and monitor themselves using a set of commonly agreed-upon standards.[1]

The US Department of Education, more formally, describes accreditation as the recognition by the federal government that an institution has attained and maintains standards required for its graduates to gain admission to other reputable institutions of higher learning or to achieve credentials for professional practice. The ultimate goal of accreditation is to ensure that education provided by institutions of higher education meets acceptable levels of quality.

American higher education accreditation had its beginnings in the late nineteenth century. New educational institutions were springing up across the country in response to the nation's rapid growth and industrialization. However, clear distinctions between the curricula of secondary and postsecondary institutions were lacking as were any agreed-on standards for collegiate study. In 1895, the first voluntary association of postsecondary institutions was formed "to define the difference between high school and college and to develop some guidelines and procedures for peer review as a condition for membership."[2]

With the increasing number of postsecondary institutions came the development of regional associations of colleges. Criteria for association membership generally required "accreditation." Accordingly, these regional associations established separate accrediting bodies or commissions that assumed the responsibility for developing standards and criteria for association membership. Regional accrediting agencies now operate in seven regions of the country. These agencies focus their reviews on colleges and universities operating in their respective regions, normally groups of contiguous states. Regional accreditation provides external validation of the quality of an institution as a whole and evaluates multiple aspects of a college or university including academic programs, mission, governance, administration, finance, resources, and other matters.[3]

In addition to validating the quality of a college or university, other important underlying objectives of accreditation are to encourage institutions to improve, facilitate the transfer of students' credits to various institutions, inform employers about the quality of education and graduates, and be responsive to the information needs of the general public.[4]

Similar to regional accrediting bodies, national accrediting agencies operate throughout the country and review institutions with a common purpose such as religious studies. National accreditation agencies started as associations of schools with similar purposes and missions. Many of these schools were not initially founded as colleges or universities but evolved into institutions of higher education as need and opportunity provided.

There are different types of national accrediting organizations including faith-based and private career. The five faith-based accreditors review religiously affiliated or doctrinally based institutions and represent a small percentage of the institutions accredited by national accrediting organizations, which in 2017 included 241 institutions and locations. The seven private career schools and programs accreditors examine and accredit 2801 institutions. There are also, finally, accrediting agencies that operate nationwide and internationally that review specific, usually single-purpose, programs.

The Congressional Research Service (CRS) provides interesting and important historic facts about the development of accreditation in the USA. According to CRS, recognition of accrediting agencies by the federal government was initiated in 1952, shortly after the passage of the Veterans' Readjustment Assistance Act of 1952, i.e., Korean G. I. Bill. The objective was to assess higher education quality and to determine which institutions would qualify to receive federal aid under the

G. I. Bill. Rather than creating its own system of quality assurance, the federal government opted to rely on existing accrediting agencies and assumed accreditation was a reliable indicator of educational quality. A recognition process was established in the Office of the US Commissioner of Education to produce a list of federally recognized accrediting agencies and associations.[5] As of March 2017, the US Department of Education recognized 36 accrediting agencies for Title IV[6] purposes. These agencies included national, regional, and programmatic accrediting organizations.[7]

Accrediting agencies are organized, connected, and operate under the general oversight of the Council of Higher Education Accreditation (CHEA). Recognizing 60 programmatic and institutional accrediting organizations, CHEA describes itself as a "national advocate and institutional voice of self-regulation of academic quality through accreditation."[8]

CHEA describes accreditation as "a trust-based, standards-based, evidence-based, peer-based process." Notwithstanding these lofty descriptors, accreditation has become one of the central concerns among critics of higher education. These concerns reached a crescendo in the late 1990s and early 2000s with many calling for major reforms or even the elimination of accreditation as a means of validating quality education. Accrediting agencies responded to some of the concerns with a shift of emphasis from inputs to outputs and outcomes, particularly student outcomes. Unfortunately, many of the concerns continue and call into question the nature, processes, and methods of American higher education accreditation as a means of validating and assuring institutional and academic quality in our nation's colleges and universities.

How Does Accreditation Work?

Initially, accreditation is sought by the candidate college or university when it has developed to a point where the leaders believe they meet the accreditation agency standards. Accreditation is *not* imposed but rather sought by colleges and universities and is viewed less as a status and more as an ongoing process of continuing improvement.

The evaluation of institutional quality is assessed through a three-step process: The first step is the self-study carried out by the college or university following guidelines of the accrediting agency. The self-study normally involves the preparation of detailed written reports showing how the institution, schools, departments, and programs determine whether it meets the agency's standards, as well as how it plans to improve in the future. The second step is the campus visit by a team of unpaid volunteer academic peers to validate the self-study and to gain an overall sense of how the institution conforms to accreditation agency standards. Visiting team members normally spread out over the campus in a predetermined manner to talk with students, faculty, staff, and administrators about the institution and the self-study. It is, in effect, a validation of the self-study and its findings.

Before leaving the campus, representatives of the team meet with and discuss their findings with the president or chief administrator of the university, school, or unit. Following their visit to an institution, the team prepares a comprehensive accreditation report that includes their findings and judgments about the strengths, weaknesses of the institution as well as its potential for improvement. The report will confirm that the university and its programs meet accreditation standards or where it failed to meet the standards and what must be done to satisfy any deficiency.

The third step in the process is the receipt of the self-study and site visit report and recommendations of the visiting team to the accreditation agency commissioners or decision-makers. The decision-making bodies of accrediting organizations determine whether accreditation should be awarded to a new institution, renewed for an existing institution, denied, or put on provisional or probationary status. All accreditation agencies have an appeals process that allows the candidate institution to question or challenge the decision of the agency.[9]

Once accreditation has been granted, periodic reviews are conducted on a regular cycle, usually every ten years. The process is labor intensive, time consuming, and costly. The cost, time, and labor required to complete the self-study have been significant concerns for decades, but little has changed in the past half century to address these concerns. Critics of the process also claim that the self-study and team visit to the campus "only demonstrates that an institution is following what the accrediting body believes to be the appropriate formula for a successful educational institution, not that it is in fact a successful institution."[10]

Considerations and Additional Concerns About Accreditation

The future of higher education in the USA is made even more uncertain by the growing concerns surrounding accreditation, what it means to students, how it impacts and assures quality of academic programs, and the increasing criticisms from Congress, colleges, universities, and the marketplace. During the past decade, higher education accreditation has witnessed a tsunami of significant criticisms. Countless papers, articles, books, and a barrage of critical media are calling into question the role and impact of what many consider the most important component of the American higher education paradigm, accreditation.

Following are some of the major concerns about American higher education accreditation.

There has always been a lingering concern about the potential or implicit conflicts of interest in the accreditation peer-review process wherein colleagues review colleagues. Many view the fact that accrediting boards and commissions as well as visiting evaluation teams are subject to the same kinds of reviews and judgments they must make about the college or university under review as an inherent weakness in the system. Critics of accreditation claim that the peer-review system employed by all regional accrediting agencies has inherent conflicts of interest that call into question the integrity of the system as well as the validity of accreditation reviews and decisions.

Correctly or incorrectly, the current system of accreditation has been described as a "kind of cartel" and gatekeeper to the billions in federal funds that flow through accredited institutions. Accreditation agency boards and commissioners, it is suggested, can protect existing accredited schools from new competitors through their entry requirements and standards. Many commissioners—perhaps the majority—are employed at institutions that their agency accredits and have vested interests in protecting those institutions.

Regional accrediting agencies are well aware of this concern and perception, and most have taken action through rigorous policies to prevent overt conflicts of interest. Even with these policies in place, CRS has pointed out "conflict of interest" as a continuing concern and suggested "Congress could explore whether a different methodology for institutional review is proper and to what extent peers may be involved in that evaluation."[11]

That has happened: US Congressman, Ron DeSantis (Florida's 6th District) introduced the Higher Education Reform and Opportunity (HERO) Act in November 2017, that seeks to bring reform to higher education by allowing individual states to develop their own systems of accrediting educational institutions, curricula, programs, and courses. The press release from Congressman DeSantis's office following the introduction of the legislation described institutions of higher education, accrediting agencies and the US Department of Education as the "iron triangle" that favors four-year degrees over practical vocational skills driving up the cost of tuition. Under the HERO Act, "All accredited programs would be eligible to receive federal student loan money."[12]

The list of other concerns is lengthy and continues to grow. A recurring concern and criticism is the failure of regional accrediting agencies and commissions to have a voice or strategy for dealing with the rising costs of higher education. Failure to address rising costs has, perhaps more than any other criticism, brought unfavorable attention to higher education and opened discussions of other problematic concerns.

Many have criticized accrediting agencies for their inability to deal effectively with advances in technology and distance learning. Being wedded to "seat-time" based credit has made it difficult for accrediting agencies to accommodate new approaches to learning that don't fit traditional metrics and academic credit system. In a similar fashion, accreditation agencies are seen by many as obstacles to innovation and slow to understand the impact of new technologies on learning and teaching. During this period of rapid technological advances, many believe effective accreditation agencies should be leading the discussions on the roles of technology in higher education, not following at great distance and seldom heard.

A common criticism that continues to grow louder is the "regional" approach to accreditation. Aside from their historical roots, what justification can be found to divide the nation's colleges and universities into seven very different, regionally based accrediting bodies? For many, regional accreditation is increasingly limited by its geographical basis at a time of increasing globalization and growing global perspective in higher education. Critics of regional geographic boundaries for accrediting bodies argue that this approach "makes little sense" in the USA and suggest a "national" approach would be more fitting and appropriate.

The critical literature also makes note of the ineffectiveness of accrediting bodies in dealing with low-performing schools and addressing the decline in several sectors of higher education. There are also those who argue that the data used by accrediting bodies to measure performance are sometimes "unintelligible" and "not comparable." Some suggest that accreditation processes are "too secretive" and argue for greater transparency. Others object to accrediting agency policy of awarding accreditation to colleges and universities that adhere to religious doctrines and philosophies that conflict with science. Similarly, others argue that accreditors are simply "too lax" and our current system is "broken." Even ardent supporters of America's accreditation admit the system is "messy" and the criticisms of the system "have merit."[13]

The volume of critical literature, media reports, conference proceedings, and other voices calling for change in American higher education accreditation continues to grow. Pressures on the current system continue to mount, and demands for change appear to be increasing. Several regional accrediting bodies have addressed some of these criticisms and concerns through competency-based credit and embracing technology-based distance education. But, for many, it is too little, too late. The concerns and criticisms have morphed into an anti-accreditation mind-set that is now taking on the character of a political movement in some sectors.

The structure and processes of the nation's higher education accreditation bodies are ripe for and in need of major reform. The slowness and inaction of accreditation agencies to fully and adequately address these issues and concerns contribute to the growing distrust of the higher education establishment. However, great care must be taken to avoid changes and reform measures that may further weaken our institutions and public confidence that sustains them.

The Bologna Process: A Model for the Future?

The Bologna Process first came to my attention in 2008 during my tenure as Provost of Zayed University in the United Arab Emirates (UAE). Zayed University had completed its application to the Middle States Higher Education Commission and self-study required for accreditation. The University had also hosted the Commission's visiting team to the campus for its review and validation of the self-study. During my first days at Zayed University, we received notification from Middle States Higher Education Commission of its decision to recognize and accredit the institution. It was, indeed, a happy time that fully justified the grand celebration hosted by the Minister of Higher Education, Sheikh Nahyan Mubarak al Nahyan.

Shortly after receiving notification of our accreditation status from Middle States, a colleague from another UAE institution came by my office to raise the question of our possible interest in becoming part of the Bologna Process. Although we chose not to pursue an affiliation with the Bologna Process countries, it introduced me to an alternative to American accreditation for ensuring quality of programs, recognizing academic degrees, and facilitating the transfer and admission of students among Bologna Process institutions.

The Bologna Process has been called a "quiet revolution in higher education."[14] Beginning in 1999 and building on common key values—freedom of expression, institutional autonomy, academic freedom, independent student unions, and free movement of students and staff—early stakeholder countries and institutions in Europe agreed to begin and to continuously adapt their national higher education systems to a new multinational model making them more compatible and strengthening their mechanisms for quality assurance.

12 Accreditation: How It Works and Is It Working? 185

A major goal of the Bologna Process was to increase student and staff mobility and facilitate employability among member systems. With 4000 institutions and 16 million students, an enterprise comparable in size and scope of higher education in the USA, the Bologna Process advanced other goals, objectives, and principles for bringing about greater convergence and integration of higher education in member countries including bringing down education borders and barriers.[15]

The following principles now guide Bologna Process members:

- International mobility of students and staff
- Autonomous higher education institutions
- Student participation in the governance of higher education
- Public responsibility for higher education
- The social dimension of the Bologna Process.

With the growth and development of the European Union, a new vision and approach to major societal and economic changes were needed in the nations' higher education systems to meet new demands and take advantage of new opportunities inherent in the increasing integration of Europe.

Responding to the challenges, Ministers of Education from 29 countries met in Bologna in 1999 to propose and agree on a common vision for higher education in Europe. This vision proved to be politically relevant for their own countries. The vision was translated into the operational goals identified in the Bologna Declaration. Following are the key elements envisioned for the European Higher Education Area (EHEA):

- European countries with different political, cultural, and academic traditions would engage in cooperation to reach a shared objective;
- European students and graduates would be able to move easily from one country to another with full recognition of qualifications and periods of study and access to the European labor market;
- European Higher Education Institutions would be able to cooperate and exchange students/staff on bases of trust and confidence and also of transparency and quality;

* European governments would fit their national higher education reforms into a broader European context;
* Higher Education in the European region would increase its international competitiveness, as well as enter into dialogue and improve cooperation with higher education in other regions of the world.[16]

Through voluntary actions and intergovernmental cooperation, the Bologna Process has, since its launch nearly twenty years ago, led to the development of the two main components of the EHEA, i.e., a common framework and common tools.

The common framework includes the overarching Framework for Qualifications of the EHEA including a common credit system (ECTS), common principles for the development of student-centered learning, the European Standards and Guidelines for Quality Assurance, a common Register of Quality Assurance Agencies, a common approach to recognition, and a common body of methodologies and sustainable achievements produced by European institutions of higher education.

The common tools include a guide for a common credit system (ECTS Users' Guide); a standardized description of the nature, level, context, content, and status of studies completed by graduates referred to as Diploma Supplement; and broad recognition of the validity of educational experiences in member countries.[17] The Bologna Process has been described as "the most far reaching and ambitious reform of higher education ever undertaken." Not only has it impacted numerous nations, languages, and cultures, it has literally turned "ancient higher education systems on their heads."[18]

The significance of the Bologna Process and the current collaboration of 48 countries is the example it sets for badly needed reform of higher education accreditation in the USA. If 29 countries—now 48—can come together and agree on common principles and methods for the operation of their systems of higher education in a way that insures academic freedom, institutional autonomy and mobility of students as well as standards of quality and quality assurance, is it not possible for the regional accrediting associations, state higher education systems, state and federal government education agencies to address the challenges facing accreditation in the USA?

The Bologna Process has attracted the attention of a few leaders in the US higher education community. Senior Vice-president of the Lumina Foundation, Holiday Hart McKiernan, argues that the USA "must adapt and apply the lessons learned from the Bologna Process if it is to increase the percentage of Americans with high quality degrees."[19] In the UK, Peter Scott, writing for The Guardian, described it as "a quiet revolution" in European higher education, "stimulated by the spirit of Bologna."[20]

Even with it's widely recognized successes, the Bologna Process has not been without its challenges. As a voluntary movement, not all member countries have fully adopted the Bologna methods. New degree structures are only partially or superficially adopted in some countries; accepting credits across borders "remains bureaucratically difficult." Student mobility—one of the goals of Bologna—has resulted in a "brain drain" from the south and east to the north and west. These limitations and other observations by Marvin Lazerson make it clear that "not everything has been successful everywhere." There have also been unanticipated consequences. The underlying belief that an "entire region within Europe and stretching into Central Asia could develop common systems of governance, finance, law, foreign relations, and higher education has essentially collapsed."[21]

Notwithstanding some of the limited successes for the entire Bologna Process region, many of the participating nations have leveraged the Bologna Process reforms into major national higher education reforms. Germany is one such example. The reforms in Germany reflect a paradigm shift of the long-standing national approach to higher education. The shift is from an "input orientation" to an "output orientation" and has embraced "competencies" rather than "hours" as a method of measuring progress toward degrees. Equally important, the Bologna Process gives the German government and universities the authority and opportunity to launch reforms in teaching and governance.[22]

The paradigmatic shift in European higher education and accreditation begs the question of what the USA can and will learn from the European reform. Many higher education observers are watching and waiting to see if the Bologna Process will have any influence on American higher education. Some claim "Europe has turned out to be an ideal laboratory from which Americans could draw lessons."

There is little optimism, however, that US higher education will look to the European model for solutions to its problems and challenges. In addition to structural factors and the multinational character of the Bologna Process, there are "national-personality factors" that will likely prevent US higher education from adopting changes modeled on the European experience.

Where does this leave US higher education with respect to learning from European experience? The American Institute for Contemporary German Studies at Johns Hopkins University attempts to answer this important question:

> Globalization increasingly forces countries to be competitive. This holds true even for a global power like the U.S. Similar to Germany, the U.S. is no longer in the position to unilaterally determine education policy, but it must instead pick up on the trends of other countries and regions in order to stay ahead of the game. In the years to come, global economic threats will force the U.S. and European higher education sectors to implement radical change. With its effectiveness in increasing the competition among both universities and countries, the Bologna model is unparalleled in its ability to bolster higher education… the European reform process has the potential to become a global template for higher education in the world's knowledge societies.[23]

There are very few signs, however, that higher education in the USA will look to the European experience as the path ahead. Indeed, there are few, if any, signs that US accreditation is looking anywhere for a model that can sustain the nation's leading role in higher education. Kevin Carey of New America Foundation sums up the view this way: "No one really likes accreditation but no one knows what else to do."

When higher education and it's accrediting bodies are unable to chart their future course, there are those who express the concern that government will step in, take the reins, and begin exerting greater controls. That may already be happening.

Conclusions and Growing Concerns

As a commissioner for one of the regional accrediting agencies, I was generally aware of the more vocal criticisms of accreditation policies and practices. I've listened to university presidents challenge the findings of the accrediting teams and argue the decisions of the commissioners. As a university provost and president, I've sat through scores of meetings as we prepared my own institutions for the rigors of the preparatory self-study followed by another year of meetings going over our findings and weaknesses as we readied the campus for the visiting accrediting team. Through all this, I found myself defending our traditional American approach to accreditation and quality assurance to colleagues in the Middle East who were convinced that the Bologna Process was the "wave of the future."

I watched from some distance the actions of the Spellings Commission and the efforts of the Bush administration to improve higher education through accreditation. I followed—again at some distance—the work of Secretary of Education, Arne Duncan, as he wrestled with the regulations and changes President Obama wanted to make in higher education. Then there were the efforts of the American Council of Trustees and Alumni to break the link between accreditation and federal funding for financial aid. Foundations—principally the Lumina Foundation and the Bill and Melinda Gates Foundation—started looking into the issues largely in response to rapidly rising costs and too few people finishing college.

None of this has escaped the attention of lawmakers in Washington, DC. Lamar Alexander, for example, is on the record along with others expressing frustration with the mounting problems in higher education and accreditation. Utah Senator Mike Lee and Florida congressman, Ron DeSantis have pushed new legislation, the HERO Act, that would break the monopolistic hold of regional accrediting bodies and give authority to states to accredit educational institutions making their students eligible for federal student loans.

Clearly, there is a widespread loss of confidence and a growing list of concerns about the role of the nation's regional higher education accreditation commissions and agencies. Pressure on the accreditation paradigm continues to build with seemingly no visible path forward. American higher education and its accrediting bodies have shown little or no interest in Europe's Bologna Process, clinging to the notion that American colleges and universities are the best in the world. The arrogance that follows this national self-image makes our current situation even more vulnerable to the weaknesses and challenges we refuse to address. Perhaps it is time to take a good look at the European model.

References

1. Doug Lederman, "No Love, But No Alternative," *Inside Higher Ed* (September 1, 2005).
2. Congressional Research Service, *An Overview of Accreditation of Higher Education in the United States* (December 12, 2014–March 23, 2017).
3. Higher Learning Commission, *Homepage.* hlcommission.org.
4. Lloyd E. Blauch, *Accreditation in Higher Education* (US Department of Health, Education, and Welfare, 1959).
5. Congressional Research Service, ibid.
6. **Title IV** is a term that refers to federal financial aid funds. Federal regulations state that any federal funds disbursed to a student's account in excess of allowable charges must be delivered to the student (or parent in case of an undergraduate PLUS loan).
7. Congressional Research Service, ibid.
8. Council of Higher Education Accreditation, *Homepage.* chea.org.
9. Congressional Research Service, ibid.
10. Ibid.
11. Ibid.
12. Ron DeSantis, Member of Congress, "DeSantis Introduces Higher Education Reform Bill," *Press Release* (November 7, 2017).
13. Linda Suskie, *Five Dimensions of Quality: A Common Sense Guide to Accreditation and Accountability* (San Francisco: Jossey-Bass, 2015), 18–21.
14. Ruth Davies, "The Bologna Process: The Quiet Revolution in Nursing Higher Education," *Nurse Education Today* (November 2008), 935–942.

15. Clifford Adelman, *The Bologna Process for U.S. Eyes: Re-learning Higher Education in the Age of Convergence* (Institute for Higher Education Policy, April 2009).
16. *The Bologna Process Revisited: The Future of the European Higher Education Area* (The Ministerial Conference, Yerevani, Armenia, 2015).
17. UNESCO, *Convention on the Recognition of Qualifications Concerning Higher Education in the European Region* (Lisbon, April 11, 1997).
18. Clifford Adelman, ibid.
19. *University World News*, September 19, 2010.
20. Peter Scott, "The Bologna Process Has Been Key to European Universities Success," *The Guardian* (April 30, 2014).
21. Marvin Lazerson, "Beyond the Bologna Process," *Chronicle of Higher Education* (April 6, 2015).
22. Tonia Bieber, *Building a Bridge Over the Atlantic? The Impact of the Bologna Process on German and U.S. Higher Education* (American Institute for Contemporary German Studies, Johns Hopkins University, December 19, 2011).
23. Ibid.

13

Attacking the Problems: Student-Centered Strategies for Governors, Governing Boards, and University Presidents

Financing public higher education in the USA with its increasing related and unrelated costs poses a formidable challenge to the sustainability of our current system. The proverbial Washington, DC metaphor of "kicking the can down the road" is one way to describe the inaction of accrediting bodies, legislative bodies, and higher education policy makers. Others could describe those responsible for our states' public higher education as "asleep at the wheel." The inevitable result of kicking the can down the road or sleeping at the wheel leaves our students and younger generation with unreasonable, unjustifiable costs and a college degree that has been measured in anachronistic credits that no longer fit or are suited for the needs and demands of the twenty-first-century workplace.

So, where do we go from here? What is our vision for the future of American public higher education? What strategies should be considered to help achieve that vision? Where is the leadership for the much needed change? And what is the agenda for change?

Tuition crisis. The path forward for a more sustainable infrastructure and future for American public higher education must first come to grips with the problem of mounting college costs and financing. The tuition crisis is crying out for strong, creative leadership in nearly every state. Many middle-class and working-class families no longer encourage their high school age children to go to college because of the high cost and knowing they are not be able to afford the tuition, room and board, and mandatory fees.

This represents a major opportunity for governors—individually and collectively—to play a meaningful leadership role in identifying options, new approaches, policies, and solutions. From a financial perspective, public higher education is at a turning point for large portions of the population. The future direction of our public colleges and universities on cost of tuition and other costs will dictate whether many aspiring young people and adults will be able to afford pursuing their education dreams.

The tuition crisis also represents an opportunity for states and Congress to come forward with creative solutions that will enable all qualified Americans to pursue their education dreams. Most students and families do not expect *free* tuition that would put the full burden on taxpayers; rather, they do look forward to a new, more reasonable approach that makes college affordable.

Academic credit: Seat time or competency? The uncertain future of higher education—public and private—places greater demands on policy makers, higher education accrediting bodies, and leaders to come to terms with the currency of higher education, i.e., the college credit and what it measures. It is increasingly clear that credit measured largely in terms of seat time and number of hours in classes is an anachronism that falls far short of the changing needs of the workplace, job market, and professions.

New models that measure or embrace "competency" and/or proficiency are needed and would be welcomed as the next iteration in the upgrading of academic credit. Such a transition would be complex and difficult for every college and university; however, the value in such a move would more than compensate all of higher education for these difficulties if the "new academic credit" actually measured knowledge, mastery of skill, or experience that leads to important job or career-related insights.

The Question of Tenure. The policy and practice of tenure, the principles of which were set forth by AAUP in 1940, occupies a prominent place in American higher education ostensibly to protect the academic freedom of faculty. The debate on the function of tenure as the best method for achieving this objective has an equally historic run and continues today. The question at the heart of the tenure debate is how do we develop and maintain the highest quality, most current and globally competitive system of higher education possible? Can that be achieved through a system that embraces the practice of tenure? A related question: Is a lifetime appointment the only tool by which we can protect academic freedom? Or, are there other means that will enable our system to protect these freedoms and not have to rely on lifetime appointments with all the disadvantages and public criticisms that come with such appointments? These questions retain currency and validity and are likely to remain important issues for the broader public, taxpayers, business and industry leaders, and higher education policy makers.

The Future of College Campuses. Among the many challenges facing higher education is the high cost of building, operating, and maintaining university campuses as historically practiced in American higher education. However, online education, with all the potential it brings for lowering the cost of higher education, is clearly an important instructional mode, now and for the future, that does not need costly campuses. In view of the new and rapidly expanding role of online technologies and their pedagogical promise, how should we view the huge investments we have made and continue to make in our university campuses? Policy makers, trustees, and university presidents have yet to come to grips with this question.

Lectures, Textbooks, and Delivering Cost-Effective Higher Education. Pillars of our higher education paradigm that served important purposes in previous times are now being called into question and may well be serious *cracks* in the structure we have relied on to support our system of public colleges and universities. For example, we know a lot more today about teaching and learning than we did even two decades ago yet we persist in using modes of instruction that our own research has shown ineffective or, at least, comparatively ineffective and costly. We allow and support publishing houses that charge totally unreasonable, even gouging prices for textbooks and are complicit in this enterprise by our continuing adoption of these overpriced texts. These costly, outmoded, ineffective tools of American higher education have a firm grip on our institutions that must be broken. There are better, more cost-effective approaches.

Oversized Administrations. The proliferation of administrative positions at nearly every major, public university is a costly fact of life in American higher education. Hundreds, if not thousands of administrative positions are added each year to the payrolls of our nation's public colleges and universities. Many of these mostly well-paid positions are not related to the academic mission but are added to ancillary functions or assistant to type roles. Closer scrutiny by university leaders and governing boards is needed more than ever to proposals or requests for creating these new positions. More importantly, governing boards need to begin questioning many of the functions now covered by the expanding number of administrative positions.

Costly Duplication of Programs and Services. State after state approves academic programs that are duplicated many times across their state system driving ever higher the cost of operating our universities. Very limited collaboration exists among colleges and universities or by our state systems. Joint ventures are almost nonexistent. It is time that we adopt an aggressively collaborative approach to meeting the academic and programmatic needs of our states and their citizens. It is good fiscal policy, good education policy, and good public policy.

Athletics. The time has come for ending student funded subsidies for intercollegiate athletics. Students and their families should no longer be required to help pay for these activities that many don't want, don't use, and can't afford. Intercollegiate athletics is, strictly speaking, not part of higher education; it is sports and entertainment. If we want to maintain these activities, and we may, we need to find another way of paying for it through expanded sponsorships, television revenue, advertising, gate receipts, and donors. Mandatory student fees, tuition revenue, and state subsidy funds are inappropriate sources for underwriting the costs of intercollegiate athletics and should be ended. Education leaders, governors, governing boards, and education policy makers could, by addressing this issue, make an immediate, significant difference that would benefit students and their families.

Presidential Compensation. A thoughtful review and new approach for setting presidential salaries are needed that is in keeping with the values and financial realities of our institutions and those for whom our institutions are created to serve, our students. A growing number of public university boards of trustees have lost an understanding of what it means to be "public" when setting the salaries of their presidents. We are violating our own values and sending the wrong message to our students, faculty, and communities when presidents' salaries are ten or twenty times larger than professor's. How can such salaries be justified when these same universities are hiring part-time, adjunct faculty to teach because there are insufficient funds to hire regular, full-time faculty? A new philosophy and mind-set are needed on presidential compensation as our universities seek to educate new generations not only through classroom instruction but through its policies, actions, and reward structures.

Demography and the Future of Student Recruitment. Education leaders, planners, and policy makers need to be watchful of the demography of our nation and the pipeline of students we seek to attract to our universities. The population characteristics of the student marketplace will be changing significantly in the next decade in ways that will require new strategies for recruitment and retention. Adult education and lifelong learning programs will become more important, even necessary, to sustain enrollments and revenue required for university operations and to meet the education needs of the changing workplace and workforce.

Reform Higher Education Accreditation. Issues surrounding America's approach to higher education accreditation continue to concern education policy makers. It is a growing concern for those whose jobs are to warrant the quality of academic programs and institutions as well as certify the transferability of academic credit to colleges and universities worldwide. Peer review or what some call "self-policing" practices and conflicts of interest—real or perceived—do not bode well for building trust in the quality of America's institutions of higher education. There are also legitimate concerns about increasing the role of the federal government in certifying quality and transferability of academic credit and all that could go wrong with that approach. This important pillar of American higher education is in need of attention and modernization. Consideration of the Bologna Process as a model for American higher education would be a useful first step in this direction and a potential, well-tested roadmap for reform.

Taken together, the issues described above are serious *cracks* in the nation's public higher education paradigm. These issues are calling out to our governors, state officials, higher education policy makers, university leaders, and boards of trustees as well as informed citizens to look for better ways, better policies, new technologies, and modalities. New approaches are needed that will enable future populations to take full advantage of all that higher education offers at a reasonable cost and not be burdened with outdated, non-related, irresponsible charges.

Unquestionably, American higher education is losing ground to other nations. While we still have many of the best colleges and universities in the world, we are increasingly vulnerable to losing our premier position internationally by our failure to recognize that the structures that sustain American higher education require immediate attention. Those closest to our colleges and universities can feel the shifting of the paradigmatic tectonic plates that have, for more than a century, provided the platform and framework for American higher education. However, the rapid pace of change, the explosion of new knowledge, the waves of new technologies, and demands for greater accountability require new thinking, courageous leadership, and greater focus on societal and workforce needs, priorities, and costs for twenty-first-century higher education.

It is time to move forward toward a new *paradigm* for public higher education in the USA, a paradigm for the twenty-first century. The new paradigm must retain the many strengths of our current higher education systems and also be open to eliminate or address its growing weaknesses, serious inefficiencies, and outright failures. The current path is not sustainable if the mission of public higher education is to provide high-quality educational opportunities to students from all socioeconomic backgrounds. But more than a new paradigm, American public higher education is in need of a new *culture*, a culture that truly puts the learning needs and interests of students first.

Agendas for Change

The formidable challenges facing American public higher education in this time of rapid change have been allowed to grow and evolve into issues impacting the affordability and very sustainability of our colleges and universities. Some of these challenges are now entrenched problems and have become "institutionalized" to a degree that major changes in policies and practices plus genuine reform will be required to resolve these concerns. Many problematic policies and practices have become the "new normal" or even a "tradition" with the result that little or no effort is expended toward resolving them. It is unfortunate for students and the many constituents of public higher education that we have allowed these dysfunctional features to become the norm and part of "life taken for granted."

This treatise has attempted to outline and briefly describe some of the more pressing, problematic issues in public higher education. Although identifying and describing these issues tend to give this work a critical, even negative tone, the major objective is quite the opposite: its purpose is to present these issues to leaders of public higher education and its chief policy makers as a fresh opportunity to review, rethink, and challenge the notion that these dysfunctional policies and practices represent the "new normal." Indeed, they do not and should not be considered "the way things are." In truth, there are many ways of lowering the cost of higher education and simultaneously improve quality. Quality does not mean "costly" despite the fact that we, as Americans, have been somewhat conditioned to think that way. Many of the ideas and suggestions presented in this work have no cost; to the contrary, some have the capacity to reduce expenditures, bring greater efficiencies, and open new opportunities for enhanced revenue.

University presidents, governing boards, and governors are confronted with a "game changing" opportunity to adopt more cost-effective, affordable, high quality, educational policies and practices.

Together, these state leaders of public higher education are in a position to create a new approach, new outlook, and a new era of collective, collaborative efforts to rewrite old dysfunctional polices and practices and replace them with new strategies that will give students and taxpayers more educational value for less cost.

Governors are in a particularly unique position to call for a fresh start in their states focused on improving public higher education and addressing those well-known and well-documented areas demanding reform. Governing boards have responsibilities for their colleges and universities and can play a significant leadership role in raising questions and requesting information related to the major issues in question. Boards of trustees, regents, and visitors have the opportunity, prerogative, and, indeed, the duty to adopt changes in policies that create more affordable, student-centered institutions.

University presidents, in their role as CEO and leader of their college or university, have significant opportunities and a moral responsibility to initiate changes to bring a more cost-effective administration to their institutions' programs, personnel, and functions. Together, governors, governing boards, and presidents are well-positioned to meet the challenges, create more affordable educational opportunities for traditional and non-traditional students, and bring a cost-conscious approach to the nation's institutions of higher education.

One of the great qualities of American higher education is the rich diversity of colleges and universities. This diversity and the unique characteristics of each institution bring with them the need for diverse and unique solutions that fit each college and university. Likewise, every state has its own history and unique approach to funding and managing public higher education. Solutions to the problems and major issues facing each state's system of higher education require recognition of this unique character. And, while there may be many similarities and common themes that run through and across public higher education in all states, there are no silver bullets nor solutions where "one size fits all." Approaches to these problems and their solutions will need to reflect the different histories, diverse institutions, and populations that make up each states' system or network of public colleges and universities.

It is possible, however, to identify targets of opportunity and a range of actions that will initiate needed change to public higher education. There are, for example, strategies that can make colleges and universities more affordable for students, increase the flexibility of institutions to adapt more quickly to changes in demands, enhance the quality of educational experiences, and better meet the needs and challenges of the ever-changing marketplace.

The following suggestions and recommendations are illustrative of strategies for initiating change and reforms in selected policies and practices in public higher education. The strategies are geared toward meeting the needs of students for a more affordable, cost-effective, quality higher education. They are also designed to address the concerns of businesses, industries, communities, states, and taxpayers.

Strategies for Governors

Governors have a huge, untapped capacity to influence the future of their states' public colleges and universities. The opportunity is there to bring about needed change, not through political force or power politics, but through persuasive leadership, listening, interacting, and being truly engaged with their higher education leaders and boards. Following are a few strategies that will help tap into this capacity for bringing positive change.

1. Visit as many campuses as possible every year for discussions with students, faculty, and administration. These visits are important substantively and symbolically. They create opportunities to listen to the concerns of students, to exchange ideas and suggestions with members of the faculty and administration, and demonstrate the importance of higher education to the governor's administration and citizens.
2. Host annual retreats for all members of university governing boards. Listen to their concerns and exchange concepts and ideas for improving access, quality, and affordability.

3. Meet periodically with university presidents as a group to listen and exchange ideas on improving access, quality, affordability, and other strategic initiatives.
4. Develop or revisit the state's strategic plan for higher education and agree on bold goals and objectives geared to the desired reforms in quality, efficiency, and affordability.
5. Explore new or expanded sources of revenue to devote to lowering cost of tuition and fees to students. Slight increases in sales, income, or other taxes would be significant sources of revenue for lowering college costs to students and would send a strong message to business and industry regarding the importance of higher education.
6. Lead an initiative in the governor's political party and legislature to assign greater importance higher education and the need lower tuition and related college/university costs while increasing efficiencies and cost-effectiveness.
7. Advocate for greater collaboration and joint ventures among public colleges and universities to reduce duplication, lower costs, expand cooperative programs, and improve quality. Such initiatives should also consider the cost/benefits of potential mergers of colleges and universities where conditions are appropriate.
8. Promote the importance among presidents and boards of trustees of the need for reducing costs, eliminating unnecessary duplication of programs and services, finding greater efficiencies, and increasing quality.
9. Work with presidents and governing boards to determine the types of expertise needed in board appointments. Timely, well-considered appointments of university trustees should be a high priority.
10. Lead the state in increasing education attainment; make education attainment a strategic goal for the state.

Strategies for Governing Boards

Governing boards and their member trustees have considerable influence in their colleges and universities and can help shape the future of their institutions. However, to be effective in bringing about change means more than just showing up at board meetings and athletic events. It means becoming a student of higher education, knowing and understanding the issues facing colleges and universities, and being willing to bring their thoughts to the table for discussion and, possibly, action. Following are some illustrative strategies for governing boards.

1. Initiate discussion and process for succession planning for major university leadership positions. Explore "best practices" that can be adopted by your board and institution. Keep in mind that this may alter past traditions and practices in filling leadership positions, e.g., president and vice presidents. Association of University Governing Boards (AGB) is a source of information and assistance.
2. Adopt a policy for executive and athletic coach compensation that keeps balance, a public perspective, the cost of student tuition and fees as well as the salaries of faculty and staff as a frame of reference.
3. Plan periodic joint retreats with Governing Boards of nearby universities with the objective of exploring potential areas of collaboration, joint ventures and reducing unnecessary duplication of programs, services, and administrative functions.
4. Discuss the professional composition and expertise needs of the board and convey those needs to the governor or individual responsible for board appointments.
5. Request a review of the institution's tenure policy and its implications for the long-term financial health and sustainability of the college or university. The review would benefit from a summary of higher education tenure policy literature that identifies the functions of tenure and options for institutions.
6. Request a review and report on the cost of textbooks and recommendations for reducing cost to students. Work with the institution's leadership and administration to lower the financial impact of textbooks while preserving needed sources for students.
7. Request a space and facilities audit or update of the latest audit with the objective of determining actual demand and use patterns of all campus facilities. Use the audit as the basis for a discussion of and planning for related topics including plans for new construction, master planning, deferred maintenance, and related issues.

8. Explore the potential of renting or leasing campus space and facilities during summer and holiday breaks to make better use of facilities and generate new revenues.
9. Encourage the development and promotion of plans for completing four-year degrees in three years. Many universities have developed models for three-year baccalaureate degrees. Request plans that might work for your institution together with the projected cost savings for students and families.
10. Request periodic reports on teaching loads and justification requirements for light loads, e.g., administrative responsibilities, special assignments, research, etc. Teaching loads and course release-time have significant cost implications that impact overall instructional costs. Develop a clear understanding of conditions under which teaching load reductions are approved and that there is a board policy for such reductions.

Strategies for University Presidents

College and university presidents are in an increasingly difficult role: On the one hand, they are expected to protect and defend the policies and practices of their institutions but, on the other hand, are also a key figure in bringing about needed changes and reforms. Presidents, alone, cannot bring the needed reforms and changes but working with their boards, governors, and community supporters can play an important and necessary catalytic role. Following are a few illustrative strategies to consider.

1. Initiate an annual, systematic, comprehensive review of student costs, cost comparisons, new costs, cost reductions, and loans incurred by students to cover costs. How do these costs compare to national student cost and loan data? Consider making this a topic of discussion and review by your administrative cabinet and governing board.
2. Launch ongoing conversations with fellow presidents to explore ways of increasing collaboration and reducing duplication,

particularly with institutions located nearby or in your geographic region. Consider making "collaboration and duplication reduction" part of the job description of one of your senior administrators.
3. Advocate for dual degree programs, early college high schools and Advanced Placement classes. Many high school students are academically qualified to enroll and compete successfully in university courses. Invest in ways to streamline and reduce time and costs for high school students coming into the college or university.
4. Initiate a candid discussion of tenure and tenure reform with the faculty senate and/or faculty unions. It may be that a mediated conversation would be good for starting the dialog. Clarify and agree on the objective of tenure, i.e., academic freedom. Investigate alternative policies that ensure academic freedom that may also increase the needed flexibility of universities to more cost-effectively meet the changing needs and academic interests of students.
5. Challenge faculty to design and propose three-year bachelor's degrees.
6. Strategically plan and implement a reduction in the size of administration. This will involve modifications in job descriptions, duties, and responsibilities. Seek new practices to reduce the negative impact of administrative bureaucracies and improve the timeliness of decisions and processes. This may well be a task that would benefit from outside expertise or consultation.
7. Request an in-depth review or detailed audit of all athletic expenditures and present the results to the governing board for their information, discussion, and possible action.
8. Consider outsourcing university services such as maintenance, grounds, transportation, etc. Compare costs on a periodic basis and present comparative information to the board for their information and possible action.
9. Review and evaluate cost and productivity of small academic programs, doctoral programs, and programs of marginal quality.
10. Open a discussion with other university presidents, higher education policy makers, and accreditation commission presidents on academic credit and what it measures. Raise questions regarding alternative measures including credit based on competency.

These "agendas for change" address the most challenging problems and issues in American public higher education. Each of the three agendas calls on those with the greatest authority and responsibility for public higher education—governors, governing boards, and presidents—to take action even if the "action" is simply opening a conversation or discussion. There are other responsible parties that can contribute to the resolutions and reforms including accrediting bodies, taxpayers, and citizens. University faculty members, faculty unions, and representative bodies such as faculty senates can be major instruments of needed change.

Each of the problems described and discussed in this treatise are well known among members of the academy. Few, if any, have been addressed: they are complex, difficult, and resist reform. Solutions will not come easy. No one individual or institution can resolve or reform these problems but, working collaboratively, the leaders of public higher education can start the process. Our collective "attitude" will be an important factor that determines our willingness to tackle these problems and persevere until we find solutions that will increase quality, lower cost and sustain one of the most important institutions in American life and society, public higher education.

Promising Prospects: Western Governor's University

I was serving as Provost at the University of Alaska Anchorage in the late 1990s when I first heard about a new university concept being discussed by some of the Western governors. Governor Roy Romer of Colorado, one of the governors leading the initiative for this new university, spoke at one of our higher education meetings and described some of the innovative features of this new university. He used concepts that were novel to most of the traditionalists sitting in the room, e.g., competency-based, online, two- or three-year degrees, low-cost, student-centered schedules and curricula and more. Like most of those listening to Governor Romer, I remember thinking this is a pretty cool idea but I can't imagine it really working with any degree of success.

Today, there are nearly 100,000 enrolled in Western Governors University and also nearly 100,000 graduates making up the alumni of this new institution.[1] High levels of student satisfaction, low cost, graduation rates that exceed most universities, and successful graduate performance in the workplace have created a positive image and reputation for this innovative university. And, more states are buying-in as the outcome metrics continue to impress education policy makers across the nation.

I sent a copy of the WGU Annual Report to a colleague and civic leader in my community who has served as a trustee at two universities and advocates for innovation in all levels of education, Pre-K through higher education. I found his response suggestive of what might well be a new perspective on our tradition-bound systems of higher education. He wrote:

> This model represents the beginning of a "self-evaluation" that all universities will have to undertake, whether they want to or not.
>
> 5 years ago Pennys and Sears thought no one would buy from Amazon .... today, Pennys and Sears are (nearly) out of business. 5 years ago, taxi drivers thought that no one could break their control on the personal transportation business. Uber changed that paradigm, almost over night.
>
> When a lower cost higher education model proves successful because employers will hire the graduates, regardless of tenured faculty, accreditation, and credit hours taken, the existing university system will lose its lock on being the only credible way to deliver higher education.[2]

For many advocates of greater innovation in higher education, Western Governors University represents a flicker of light at the end of the increasingly dark tunnel that most public universities find themselves in. The model, after nearly twenty years of operation, is concluding a successful proof-of-concept period and is now entering a new period of widespread acceptance by states and anticipated growth.

New models and innovations in public higher education are possible. One of the important lessons we are learning from the WGU experiment is the powerful role that governors can and should play in addressing the problems and looming crises facing our colleges and universities.

WGU represents a substantial paradigm shift and promising example of outstanding gubernatorial leadership in higher education that can and should be replicated in the months and years ahead.

References

1. Western Governors University, Annual Report, 2017.
2. Dr. Tom Brady, email, June 30, 2018, quoted with permission.

14

Epilogue: Theoretical Perspectives on Change

How are we to understand, explain, and address the challenges facing American higher education? What forces and factors are producing the problems that most of our nation's public colleges and universities are facing? Are there theoretical perspectives or frameworks that might allow us to do a better job of understanding and forecasting the future of higher education? How might we, as a community of scholars and researchers, approach our own institutions as objects of study to gain a better understanding of how to plan strategically, set policy, function effectively and efficiently, work collaboratively, and meet the higher education needs of our students, communities, states, and the nation? Do we even know what those higher education needs will be in five, ten, or twenty years?

There is no shortage of explanations for the changes, challenges, and crises taking place in American higher education. Policy makers, university presidents, politicians, parents, journalists, students, and everyday taxpayers have offered their views and explanations. Some of these explanations are well formulated and are based on logic and empirical data. However, the best that can be said about some explanations is that they are partial explanations, have limited validity, and overlook many important factors. Still other explanations are little more than guesses concocted from media reports, personal experience, or even conspiracy theories.

A review of the scholarly, professional, media and popular literature on higher education over the past twenty years leaves one with clear sense of several themes running through the wide-ranging explanations for the concerns and challenges facing our nation's colleges and universities. Some of these themes fit reasonably well with one or more of the many theories of institutions and social change. A major problem, however, is the lack of a unified theory of higher education that can guide research and provide a framework for interpreting the data and findings from our studies. Higher education, as a broad and complex enterprise, is in need of more holistic research and a theoretical basis to help guide and interpret that research. Much of the research and even popular study of higher education has focused on very limited, specific issues such as "tuition," "enrollment," or "athletics." While important and not to be discouraged, the real frontier in the study of higher education is how these limited, specific issues and problems relate to one another and how, together and interacting, contribute to the whole institution or enterprise. What we currently have in the way of theory is akin to a 1000 piece jigsaw puzzle; each piece represents a particular feature of higher education and each of the pieces has its own particular theoretical character. The need—indeed, the task ahead—is to bring together these numerous and varied theoretical perspectives into a multiple theoretical framework that is more holistic and embraces the multiple functions, structures, processes, interactions, and outcomes that characterize the higher education enterprise.

In an effort to move toward a multiple theoretical framework for guiding future research, this Epilogue suggests some theoretical starting points. The following selection of theories offers policy analysts and students of American higher education an illustrative framework for understanding the current dynamics at work in our nation's colleges and universities.

Classic sociological theories—functionalism, conflict, and symbolic interactionism—have played an important role in guiding research and building a knowledge base on a wide range of issues in higher

14 Epilogue: Theoretical Perspectives on Change 211

education. Research from a functionalist perspective tends to focus on ways higher education prepares students for careers in one of the professions. The emphasis in recent years on "outcomes" of higher education fits neatly into a functionalist perspective. Others may be interested in the *latent* functions of higher education and look at the ways in which our colleges and universities serve to bring people together and foster better understanding of different cultures and backgrounds. Or, still others may be interested in understanding the latent function of higher education with respect to its economic impact on the local economy.

Conflict theorists would be more likely to focus on ways higher education, or the lack thereof, emphasizes or reinforces inequalities in society, i.e., social classes and class conflict. Researchers approaching their study from a conflict perspective would be interested in those aspects of higher education that help perpetuate social inequality, e.g., differences between an "Ivy League" education versus a community college education. Questions of how the relative power and resources of different groups and classes influence outcomes or the quality of higher education would be of special interest to conflict theorists.

Researchers approaching their study from a symbolic interactionist perspective would tend to focus on the interactions that take place on college and university campuses such as student–professor relationships, administration–faculty interactions, and gender relationships. Symbolic interactionist researchers would have a special interest in the *meanings* of various experiences and events for the different constituencies of our higher education institutions. Studies of expectations and attitudes would figure largely into the symbolic interactionist's perspective and research.

Max Weber's theory of bureaucracy would fit a wide range of major issues facing major universities and systems of higher education. Weber, a nineteenth-century German sociologist, was the first to use and describe the term bureaucracy. Bureaucracies, he argued, are fair and efficient systems for operating large organizations. In bureaucracies, there is a clear division of labor and well-defined job descriptions for each of its members. One of the major issues in public higher education is the growth and size of the higher education bureaucracies in nearly every state. Weber's theory of bureaucracy would lend itself to the study of the large organizations and systems that have evolved to support higher education.

Political theory has much to offer the study of higher education. Although there are some variations and different schools of thought in political theory, the general utility of their theoretical propositions for understanding key aspects of higher education is widely recognized. Issues such as legitimacy, power, equality, democracy, regulation, rule of law, authority, and justice fit neatly into the study and understanding of higher education.

Other perspectives and frameworks include theories of social change, e.g., evolutionary theory, cyclical theory, economic theory, and technological theory. From the business world, there are theories of marketing and competition that are also relevant to many of the functions of higher education. Institutional theory may have a high degree of relevance to the current concerns and challenges of higher education.

These brief descriptions of several theoretical perspectives and their relevance to higher education are illustrative of a much larger body of theories that can broaden our understanding of American higher education. The multiple perspectives and diversity of theoretical frameworks provide a starting point for the development of a more unified unified theory or meta-theory of higher education that, if developed, will enable scholars, policy analysts, and leaders to better understand their institutions and forecast the outcomes of their policies and actions.

Clearly, there is a great need for a better understanding of the nation's institutions of higher education, both private and public. This need should drive a much larger, more comprehensive program of research to help us achieve this understanding. It is also important that this research be couched in theoretical frameworks or perspectives that lend a more holistic recognition and appreciation of our institutions and the complex interactions among the many parts that occur every day. Without this understanding, our policies, programs, and priorities could easily fall short of their intended objectives or may even work against our values, missions, and goals, i.e., unintended consequences.

It is hoped that this history, background, and perspective on the many daunting challenges facing American higher education summarized in this treatise will stimulate creative solutions, open new doors and windows for more theoretically based research and a greater holistic understanding of higher education. Further, it is my hope that our current and future research will inform policies and actions that will alter our current and will lead to a more certain student-centered and sustainable future, a future that, first and foremost, truly serves the needs and interests of twenty-first-century students, their families, our communities, and the nation.

Bibliography

Altbach, Philip G., Patricia J. Gumport, and D. Bruce Johnstone (eds.), *In Defense of American Higher Education* (Baltimore: The Johns Hopkins University Press, 2001).
Block, Walter, *Labor Economics from a Free Market Perspective* (New Jersey: World Scientific, 2008).
Bok, Derek, *Beyond the Ivory Tower: Social Responsibilities of the Modern University* (Cambridge, MA: Harvard University Press, 1982).
Brown, David (ed.), *University Presidents as Moral Leaders* (Westport, CT: Praeger Publishers, 2006).
Chait, Richard P., *The Questions of Tenure* (Cambridge, MA: Harvard University Press, 2002).
Cole, Jonathan R., *Toward a More Perfect University* (New York: Public Affairs- Member of the Perseus Book Group, 2016).
Crowley, Joseph N., *No Equal in the World: An Interpretation of the Academic Presidency* (Reno: University of Nevada Press, 1994).
Dickeson, Robert C., *Prioritizing Academic Programs and Services: Reallocating Resources to Achieve Strategic Balance* (San Francisco, CA: Jossey-Bass, 1999).
Duderstadt, James J., *A University for the 21st Century* (Ann Arbor: University of Michigan Press, 2000).

Duderstadt, James J., Daniel E. Atkins, and Douglas Van Houweling, *Higher Education in the Digital Age: Technology Issues and Strategies for American Colleges and Universities* (Westport, CT: Praeger Publishers, 2002).
Duderstadt, James J., and Farris W. Womack, *The Future of the Public University in America: Beyond the Crossroads* (Baltimore and London: The Johns Hopkins University Press, 2003).
Ehrenberg, Ronald G., *Tuition Rising: Why College Costs So Much* (Cambridge, MA: Harvard University Press, 2000).
Etzkowitz, Henry, *The Triple Helix: University-Industry-Government Innovations in Action* (New York and London: Routledge, 2008).
Fairweather, James S., *Faculty Work and Public Trust: Restoring the Value of Teaching and Public Service in American Academic Life* (Boston: Allyn and Bacon, 1996).
Foray, Dominique, *The Economics of Knowledge* (Cambridge, MA: The MIT Press, 2006).
Gilley, J. Wade, *Thinking About American Higher Education: The 1990s and Beyond* (New York: American Council on Education and Macmillan, 1991).
Hanna, Donald E., *Higher Education in an Era of Digital Competition: Choices and Challenges* (Madison, WI: Atwood Publishing, 2000).
Kennedy, Donald, *Academic Duty* (Cambridge, MA: Harvard University Press, 1997).
King, Roger, Simon Marginson, and Rajani Naidoo (eds.), *Handbook on Globalization and Higher Education* (Cheltenham: Edward Elgar Publishing Limited, 2011).
Kuhn, Thomas S., *The Structure of Scientific Revolutions* (Chicago: The University of Chicago Press, 1962).
Lynton, Ernst A., and Sandra E. Elman, *New Priorities for the University* (San Francisco: Jossey-Bass, 1987).
Massey, William F., *Honoring the Trust: Quality and Cost Containment in Higher Education* (Bolton, MA: Anker Publishing Company, 2003).
McGee, Jon, *Breakpoint: The Changing Marketplace for Higher Education* (Baltimore: The Johns Hopkins University Press, 2015).
McMillin, Linda A., and William G. Berberet (eds.), *New Academic Compact: Revisioning the Relationship Between Faculty and Their Institutions* (Bolton, MA: Anker Publishing Company, 2002).
Mestenhauser, Josef A., and Brenda J. Ellingboe, *Reforming the Higher Education Curriculum: Internationalizing the Campus* (Phoenix, AZ: The Onyx Press, 1998).

Neusner, Jacob, and Noam M. M. Neusner, *Reaffirming Higher Education* (New Brunswick: Transaction Publishers, 2000).

Peek, Graham, *Mission and Change: Institutional Mission and Its Application to the Management of Further and Higher Education* (Buckingham: The Society for Research in Higher Education, 1994).

Pelikan, Jaroslav, *The Idea of the University: A Reexamination* (New Haven and London: Yale University Press, 1992).

Perna, Laura W., and Joni E. Finney, *The Attainment Agenda: State Policy Leadership in Higher Education* (Baltimore: The Johns Hopkins University Press, 2014).

Rowley, Daniel James, Herman D. Lujan, and Michael G. Dolence, *Strategic Choices for the Academy* (San Francisco: Jossey-Bass, 1998).

Selingo, Jeffrey J., *College (Un)Bound: The Future of Higher Education and What It Means for Students* (Boston: New Harvest, 2013).

Seymour, Daniel, *Once Upon a Campus: Lessons for Improving Quality and Productivity in Higher Education* (Phoenix, AZ: American Council on Education and Oryx Press, 1995).

Shulman, James L., and William G. Bowen, *The Game of Life: College Sports and Educational Values* (Princeton and Oxford: Princeton University Press, 2001).

Smith, Page, *The Quiet Crisis: How Higher Education Is Failing America* (Bolton, MA: Anker Publishing Company, 2014).

Smith, Page, *Killing the Spirit: Higher Education in America* (New York: Viking Penguin, 1990).

Solomon, Robert, and Jon Solomon, *Up the University: Re-creating Higher Education in America* (Reading, MA: Addison-Wesley Publishing Company, 1993).

Sutton, Susan Buck, and Daniel Obst (eds.), *Developing Strategic International Partnerships: Models for Initiating and Sustaining Innovative Institutional Linkages* (New York: Institute of International Education, 2011).

Tinto, Vincent, *Leaving College: Rethinking the Causes and Cures of Student Attrition*, 2nd ed. (Chicago: The University of Chicago Press, 1993).

Trani, Eugene P., and Robert D. Holsworth, *The Indispensable University: Higher Education, Economic Development and the Knowledge Economy* (Lanham: Rowman and Lilttlefield, 2010).

Index

A

Academic calendar 65, 75, 82–84, 87
Academic credit 28, 31, 38, 83, 182, 194, 197, 198, 205
Academic freedom 43–47, 50, 51, 53–57, 164, 184, 186, 195, 205
Accountability 15, 17, 30, 53, 54, 119, 157–160, 164, 170–173, 198
Accreditation 7, 38, 99, 175–184, 186–190, 197, 205, 207
Administration(s) 2, 6, 15–17, 20, 21, 27, 44, 53, 64, 66, 75, 85–87, 91, 92, 97, 99, 125, 129, 135, 147, 168, 169, 173, 178, 189, 196, 200, 201, 203, 205, 211

Admissions 19, 30, 31, 83, 114, 119, 142, 144, 145, 177, 184
Adult student(s) 147–149
Agarwal, Anant 67, 72
Amenities 13, 15, 19, 20, 64, 133, 149
war 19
Anomalies 3, 4, 6–8
Anthony, James Soto 66
Arbesman, Samuel 52
Associations 4, 7, 8, 46, 53, 81, 87, 110, 128, 167, 169, 172, 177–179, 186
Athletes 106, 109, 111, 113–119
pay 116, 119
preferential treatment 113–115
Athletic directors 106, 108
Autonomy 37, 161, 163–165, 170, 171, 173, 175, 184, 186

Auxiliary enterprises 21

B

Baldwin, Roger G. 47
Bennett hypothesis 18, 19
Bergmann, Barbara R. 15
Block, Walter E. 49
Boards 23, 24, 38, 62–64, 66, 71,
    73, 79, 80, 82, 87, 93, 97, 98,
    100, 102, 105, 108, 109, 126,
    128–131, 133, 134, 136, 137,
    144, 148, 157, 159, 163–170,
    173, 181, 194, 196, 199–206
    of trustees 16, 38, 48, 62, 63, 82,
    102, 131, 135, 137, 146, 154,
    157, 159, 160, 166, 168, 169,
    172, 177, 197, 198, 200, 202
Bok, Derek 171, 172
Bologna Process 35–37, 184–190,
    198
Bowen, William G. 62, 119

C

Campus(es) 2, 4, 7, 16, 17, 20, 34,
    48, 53, 57, 59–73, 79, 82, 86,
    88, 91, 92, 94, 101, 109, 111,
    113, 115, 116, 118, 127, 128,
    131, 133–135, 137, 138, 141,
    144, 147–149, 152, 153, 166,
    170, 180, 184, 189, 195, 201,
    203, 204, 211
Carnegie, Andrew 29–35
Carnegie Unit 30–33, 38, 39
Chait, Richard 56
Challenge(s) 1–6, 8, 9, 17, 31, 32,
    37, 39, 44, 46, 48, 49, 57, 61,
    62, 65, 71–73, 84, 85, 94–96,
    99, 103, 104, 106, 113,
    116–118, 125, 126, 128–135,
    138, 142–146, 148, 154, 157,
    158, 160, 165, 167–169,
    171–173, 180, 185, 187–190,
    193, 195, 199–201, 205, 209,
    210, 212
China 152, 153
Chorister, Jay L. 47
Christensen, Clayton 73
Clotfelter, Charles T. 48
Coaches, salaries 7, 13, 17, 29, 43,
    44, 49, 51, 55, 86, 107–109,
    111, 114, 119, 132–134, 197,
    203
Cole, Jonathan R. 50, 62, 138
Collaboration 44, 93, 100–102, 104,
    186, 196, 202–205
Collaborative leadership 100
Collective vision viii, ix
Collins, Jim 137
Community college(s) 17, 69, 83,
    98, 99, 145, 211
Competency-based 35, 59, 73, 83,
    183, 206
Competition 12, 19, 61, 70, 98,
    106, 130, 142, 150, 188, 212
Comte, Auguste 141
Congress 8, 22, 50, 133, 181, 182,
    194
Constitution 158, 160–164
Cost-effective 5, 47, 55, 67, 81, 82,
    87, 102, 195, 196, 199–202,
    205
Crises 8, 125, 137, 142, 207, 209
Curricula, curriculum 4, 29, 60, 92,
    94, 96, 101, 177, 182, 206

Index

D

Dean(s) 7, 17, 44, 91, 92, 97, 100, 112, 125, 127, 137, 175
Debt 13, 14, 19, 22–24, 61, 62, 70, 80, 105
Decision-making 14, 96, 128, 167, 170, 180
Deferred maintenance 62, 69–71, 133, 203
Degree 11–13, 23, 27, 28, 30, 35–37, 39, 45, 52, 55, 60, 67, 83, 84, 93, 94, 98, 99, 101, 103, 112, 141, 145–148, 150, 163, 167, 187, 193, 199, 205, 206, 212
   four-year 84, 98, 99, 112
Degree qualifications framework 35
Department chairs 92, 112, 175
Dickeson, Robert C. 96, 98
Diversity 64, 124, 131, 137, 146, 152, 154, 200, 212
Donors 1, 2, 16, 95, 167, 168, 196
The Drake Group 118, 119
Dropout rate 11, 143
Dropout(s) 11, 143
Drucker, Peter 61
Duderstadt, James 15, 66, 68, 167, 168
Duplication 16, 91–96, 98, 100–104, 164, 196, 202–205
   programs 93–95, 98, 101–103, 202
   services 16, 17, 91, 92, 96, 101–103, 196, 202, 203

E

Economics 3, 13, 15, 47, 50, 60–62, 64, 65, 72, 94, 105
   of tenure 47, 50–52

Economy 1, 5, 15, 23, 30, 33, 34, 37, 39, 40, 131, 162, 211
Education 1–9, 11–24, 27–40, 43–47, 51–57, 59–69, 71–73, 75, 77–82, 84–88, 91–93, 95–100, 102–104, 110–113, 117, 119, 120, 123–132, 134, 135, 137, 138, 141–154, 157–167, 169–173, 175–179, 181–190, 193–203, 205–213
Ehrlich, Thomas 33
Eliot, Charles 29, 31
Enrollment 19–21, 44, 67, 72, 103, 143, 144, 152–154, 210
Entrepreneur 15
Executive search firms 129
Eyring, Henry J. 73

F

Faculty senate 53, 128, 169, 205, 206
Fees 4, 11, 20, 23, 61, 71, 75, 87, 97, 108, 110–113, 116, 119, 133, 148, 153, 194, 196, 202, 203
   mandatory 12, 23, 72, 75, 80, 108, 110, 112, 113, 115, 116, 119, 133, 148, 194, 196
Fiduciary 51, 159, 168, 169
   duty 168
   responsibilities 11, 51
Financial aid 17–19, 30, 32, 81, 147, 149, 189

G

Globalization 53, 183, 188

Governance 7, 94, 131, 157–161, 163–166, 169, 170, 172, 173, 178, 185, 187
Governing board(s) 17, 20, 24, 64, 66, 71, 87, 97, 98, 102, 105, 108, 109, 126, 129, 130, 134, 157, 159, 163, 167–170, 199–206
Graduate, student(s) 12, 36, 77
Graduation 11, 12, 30, 31, 84, 94, 117, 144, 145, 148, 150, 176, 207

H

Harris, John 28
Holistic governance 160, 164

I

Indebtedness 12, 23, 24, 97, 133
India 152, 153
Inflation 4, 12, 13, 15, 80, 81, 112
Infrastructure 2, 4–8, 27, 38, 61, 72, 99, 104, 110, 153, 173, 193
Intercollegiate 105–107, 109–114, 116–120, 196
  athletics 105–107, 109–113, 116–120, 196, 210
  sports 105, 109, 110, 112, 116–118, 196
International student(s) 146, 151–153, 155

K

Kauvar, Gerald 84, 135
Knight Commission 105, 110, 117–119

Knowledge economy 5, 39
Kuhn, Thomas 2, 3, 6

L

Leader 66, 135, 200, 207
leadership 66, 134
Lecture(s) 46, 52, 53, 67, 73, 75–79, 87, 195
Legislature(s) 1, 14, 16, 17, 23, 24, 34, 51, 54, 64, 65, 71, 100, 102, 108, 119, 133, 158–160, 202
Lowell, Abbott R. 31
Lumina Foundation 36, 37, 150, 187, 189

M

Marketplace 4, 9, 24, 37, 68, 73, 105, 146, 181, 197, 201
Mazur, Eric 76, 78
McGee, Robert W. 49, 51, 55, 56
Media 1, 4, 21, 106, 107, 109, 110, 114, 116, 135, 154, 181, 183, 210
Merisotis, Jamie 36, 37, 150
Moral leadership 134–138
Morrison, Gail M. 103

N

National Collegiate Athletic Association (NCAA) 105–107, 114, 116–119
Nguyen, Tuan 61
Non-traditional student(s) 60, 83, 144, 147–151, 200

Index

O

Outcomes, assessment 3, 22, 23, 32, 35–37, 49, 54, 75, 79, 100, 106, 107, 127, 145, 146, 157, 159, 175, 176, 179, 210–212

P

Paradigm 2–9, 23, 24, 37, 38, 40, 61, 62, 65, 67, 68, 82, 95, 99, 103, 120, 173, 181, 187, 190, 195, 198, 208
Peer review 177, 197
Policy(ies) 1, 2, 4, 5, 7, 8, 12, 15–17, 21–24, 28, 30, 33, 35, 43–45, 47–50, 53, 54, 56, 57, 61, 62, 65, 67, 72, 73, 75, 92–97, 102, 103, 110, 116, 118, 128, 131, 132, 137, 141, 144, 145, 149, 150, 152–155, 157, 158, 160, 164–166, 169–172, 182, 183, 188, 189, 194–201, 203–205, 207, 209, 210, 212, 213
  education 2, 4, 5, 7, 12, 15–17, 23, 24, 33, 35, 44, 57, 61, 62, 67, 73, 75, 92, 93, 95, 97, 110, 131, 141, 145, 150, 154, 157, 158, 166, 171, 172, 183, 188, 193–196, 198, 199, 203, 207, 209, 213
  fiscal 48, 50, 92, 95, 97, 196
  public 15, 17, 28, 43, 62, 91, 92, 95, 96, 110, 157, 158, 160, 165–167, 170, 171, 193, 194, 199, 200, 203
Population 4, 6, 9, 11, 19, 81, 141–145, 147–154, 194, 197, 198, 200

Population projections 142
Post-tenure review 53, 54
Poverty 11, 107
Presidential 22, 117, 126, 127, 129, 130, 132, 133, 136, 137, 197
  compensation 126, 132, 133, 197
  salaries 132, 133, 197
  selection 126, 127, 129–131
Pressures 1, 3–5, 11, 49, 61, 67, 68, 99, 100, 159, 161, 183
Priorities 15, 85, 87, 95, 96, 105, 164, 168, 198, 212
Programs 4, 7, 8, 12–14, 19, 24, 78, 91–103, 106–110, 112–114, 118, 120, 128, 129, 141, 148–150, 164, 169, 170, 172, 177, 178, 180–182, 184, 196, 197, 200, 202, 203, 205, 212
  academic 24, 78, 93–96, 100–103, 107, 108, 113, 114, 120, 177, 178, 181, 184, 205
Provost(s) 7, 44, 53, 61, 78, 86, 92, 97, 100, 125, 127, 130, 137, 184, 189, 206
Public opinion 3, 4, 51, 138

R

Redundant 15, 20
Regents 100, 159, 160, 166, 167, 200
Reich, Robert 15
Revenue 14, 15, 22, 97, 107–110, 133, 138, 152, 153, 196, 197, 199, 202, 204
  sources 14, 97, 108, 110, 202
Ridpath, David 107
Romer, Roy (Governor) 206

S

Saudi Arabia 152
Scandals 106, 109, 116, 117, 135, 137
Schulman, Lee 33
Self-study 175, 180, 184, 189
Shulman, James L. 32, 119
Smith, Paul 78
State(s) 2, 11–17, 19, 22, 23, 27, 28, 35, 37, 38, 47, 49, 50, 54, 57, 62, 64, 65, 69–71, 86, 91–93, 95–101, 103, 104, 106, 107, 111, 112, 118, 119, 123, 126, 132–134, 142, 154, 158–167, 171–173, 175, 176, 178, 182, 184, 186, 189, 194, 196, 198, 200–202, 207, 209, 211
Strategic planning 96, 127, 154
Student-centered 78, 87, 186, 200, 206, 213
Student loans 11, 12, 18, 21, 22, 97, 113, 133, 147, 189
Subsidies 4, 18, 22, 23, 34, 49, 51, 97, 110–113, 165, 196
  state 22, 23, 34, 49, 51, 97, 165
Succession planning 127, 129–131, 203
Sustainability 1, 2, 6, 8, 20, 51, 102, 105, 157–163, 165, 167, 193, 199, 203

T

Taxpayers 17, 44, 51, 70, 71, 92, 95, 96, 101–103, 107, 134, 146, 160, 164, 167, 171, 172, 176, 194, 195, 200, 201, 206, 209

Teaching 7, 16, 29–33, 45, 48–50, 52, 55, 62, 65–67, 76–79, 110, 119, 125, 182, 187, 195, 204
  methods 4, 52, 77, 79
Technologies 3, 13, 33, 35, 53, 62, 64–68, 70, 83, 158, 164, 173, 182, 195, 198
  information 64
Textbooks 7, 75, 77, 80–82, 87, 195, 196, 203
Theory, unified 16, 52, 210–212
Tower, Cathy A. 53
Trachtenberg, Steven 84, 129, 136
Trakman, Leon 172
Trimester 82, 83
Trustees 16, 38, 49, 51, 53, 62, 63, 73, 82, 87, 92, 93, 102, 117–119, 126–131, 135–137, 146, 154, 157, 166–169, 172, 177, 189, 195, 197, 198, 200, 202
Tuition 4, 7, 11, 13–15, 17–23, 51, 60, 61, 69, 71, 72, 75, 79, 80, 87, 95–97, 99, 108, 110–112, 133, 138, 143, 148, 153, 182, 193, 194, 196, 202, 203, 210
Tuition crisis 21
Tuning USA 37

U

Undergraduate(s) 12, 64, 76, 81, 84, 103, 112, 146

Index   225

V
Vedder, Richard 85

W
Wall Street 21, 24
Western Governors University 207

Workforce 4, 9, 23, 30, 37, 39, 46,
    49, 54, 86, 148, 150, 159,
    161, 162, 166, 197, 198

Z
Zayed University 184